T0334275

Gender and Corporate Governance

Gender diversity as a corporate governance mechanism is high on the agenda for regulators, firms, and researchers. Particularly, gender board composition has received a great deal of attention in recent years. The theoretical foundations of the benefits associated with the inclusion of female directors on boards, how to measure gender diversity in the boardroom, and its real impact on board decisions and firm strategies remain hotly debated. Drawing on empirical data, this book summarises the current situation regarding gender board diversity and provides a concise overview of the most important concerns about this topic.

This will be a vital tool to guide the future debate on gender diversity and corporate governance for researchers and advanced students, as well as regulators, policy-makers, and board members.

Francisco Bravo-Urquiza is Associate Professor at the Department of Accounting and Financial Economics in the University of Seville, Spain. He has a PhD in business administration. His research focuses on information disclosure, corporate governance, board of directors, and gender diversity. He has also participated in research in several projects funded by the Ministry of Science and Innovation of Spain.

Nuria Reguera-Alvarado is Associate Professor of Accounting at the Faculty of Economics and Business Administration of the University of Seville, Spain. She has a PhD in business administration. Her research focuses on corporate governance, earnings management, gender diversity, and audit. She also has participated in research in several projects funded by the Ministry of Science and Innovation of Spain.

Routledge Focus on Accounting and Auditing

Advances in the fields of accounting and auditing as areas of research and education, alongside shifts in the global economy present a constantly shifting environment. This presents challenges for scholars and practitioners trying to keep up with the latest important insights in both theory and professional practice. Routledge Focus on Accounting and Auditing presents concise texts on key topics in the world of accounting research.

Individually, each title in the series provides coverage of a key topic in accounting and auditing, whilst collectively, the series forms a comprehensive collection across the discipline of accounting.

The Boundaries in Financial and Non-Financial Reporting
A Comparative Analysis of their Constitutive Role
Laura Girella

The Future of Auditing
David Hay

Accounting Regulation in Japan
Evolution and Development from 2001 to 2015
Masatsugu Sanada and Yoshihiro Tokuga

Gender and Corporate Governance
Francisco Bravo-Urquiza and Nuria Reguera-Alvarado

For more information about the series, please visit www.routledge.com/ Routledge-Focus-on-Accounting-and-Auditing/book-series/RFAA

Gender and Corporate Governance

Francisco Bravo-Urquiza and
Nuria Reguera-Alvarado

Routledge
Taylor & Francis Group

LONDON AND NEW YORK

First published 2020
by Routledge
2 Park Square, Milton Park, Abingdon, Oxon OX14 4RN

and by Routledge
52 Vanderbilt Avenue, New York, NY 10017

Routledge is an imprint of the Taylor & Francis Group, an informa business

First issued in paperback 2021

© 2020 Francisco Bravo-Urquiza and Nuria Reguera-Alvarado

British Library Cataloguing-in-Publication Data
A catalogue record for this book is available from the British Library

Library of Congress Cataloging-in-Publication Data
Names: Bravo-Urquiza, Francisco, author. |
Reguera-Alvarado, Nuria, author.
Title: Gender and corporate governance / Francisco Bravo-Urquiza
and Nuria Reguera-Alvarado.
Description: Abingdon, Oxon ; New York, NY : Routledge, 2020. |
Series: Routledge focus on accounting and auditing |
Includes bibliographical references and index.
Identifiers: LCCN 2019043426 (print) | LCCN 2019043427 (ebook) |
Subjects: LCSH: Boards of directors. | Women directors of corporations. |
Corporate governance. | Sex discrimination.
Classification: LCC HD2745 .B65 2020 (print) |
LCC HD2745 (ebook) | DDC 658.4/22082–dc23
LC record available at https://lccn.loc.gov/2019043426
LC ebook record available at https://lccn.loc.gov/2019043427

ISBN: 978-0-367-20929-2 (hbk)
ISBN: 978-1-03-208349-0 (pbk)
ISBN: 978-0-429-26420-7 (ebk)

Typeset in Times New Roman
by Newgen Publishing UK

Contents

Illustrations

Figures

Tables

Preface

The participation of women and men in the global economy remains unequal. The situation is clearly graver in emerging economies, but developed countries are not exempt from inequalities, which persist in many different fields. Accordingly, issues regarding gender diversity have generated a great deal of attention in recent years for regulators, politicians, professionals, and society in general. One proof of this is the repercussion of this topic on the Internet. For instance, a quick search including the terms "gender diversity" leads to millions of results. In particular, although currently the majority of women are employed and the number of graduate women exceeds men, and despite the regulatory and societal pressures, progress on gender diversity at work seems to have stalled, especially in top management positions. And inequalities remain in both the public and the private spheres.

The achievement of gender equality in leadership positions has been precisely one of the major challenges in recent years. Many voices call for the need to increase the presence of women in decision-making structures in order to make a real step towards gender equality. "Men still run the world; I'm not sure it's going so well". This was said by Sheryl Sandberg, Chief Operating Officer of Facebook, in the Annual Meeting in Davos in 2016; but this idea has become widespread, and large streams of thought advocate the inclusion of women in structures of power, which undoubtedly would mean significant efforts from many different spheres. On the other side, there are also detractors who criticise the pressures to raise female representation in organs of power. In this scenario, a crucial question has been repeatedly asked: is it necessary to include more women in decision-making positions?

To tackle all the aspects related to gender diversity and equality is beyond the scope of this book. This project specifically aims at describing the situation concerning women in the corporate governance structures of firms, particularly in the boardroom. Given the authority of boards of directors, this has become a hot topic, and researchers all over the world have increasingly tried to find out whether the appointment of women to a board may contribute to business success or if it is only explained by social and moral reasons. Anyway, fairness regarding the participation of women in leadership positions is vital to point out gender equality. In this sense, this issue has remained in the political agenda in a number of countries.

Moving more towards specifics, this book is divided into several chapters, starting with an introduction regarding women and governance in general, where general issues concerning gender diversity in boards of directors are especially highlighted. Chapter 2 provides an overview about the participation of women in the business world, giving a run down on the barriers traditionally found by women. Chapter 3 addresses the regulations and the situation regarding gender diversity in boards of directors. Next, Chapter 4 contains a summary of the main theoretical approaches employed to justify the participation of women in boards. Chapter 5 moves on to methodological aspects and aims to explain the measures commonly employed for gender diversity in the boardroom. Chapter 6 summarises the results from the empirical evidence on gender board composition, especially underlining the findings about the effect of gender board diversity on different firm outcomes. Finally, Chapter 7 provides the main conclusions of the book and some personal considerations.

Therefore, this book may be useful for students in graduate and postgraduate programmes, who can comprehend the dimension of this subject and enhance their awareness of gender diversity issues. We also intend to provide information that can serve professional bodies (i.e., international policy-makers on corporate governance) to improve their understanding about gender diversity in board positions. In addition, we expect the book to contribute to researchers from several disciplines (management, business, ethics, and finance, among others), thereby providing a big picture about theoretical approaches, methodologies, and the current status of empirical evidence concerning gender board composition. This book does not use particularly complex scientific language, so the general public could also benefit from reading it.

The authors have previously done research on gender issues and think this book is an opportunity to put together relevant ideas regarding gender in corporate governance structures. At the same time, it is also timely to increase the visibility of women in top business positions, especially now, when society is particularly sensitive to gender concerns and current mainstreams have emphasised the gender gap in governance structures. The authors hope the readers enjoy the book and benefit from reading it.

The authors would also like to acknowledge the support provided by the Spanish Ministry of Economy and Competitiveness [Projects ECO2015-69637-R].

1 Women and governance

This section underlines the ongoing debates concerning the need for enhancing female participation in governance structures, which are responsible for top-level decisions in both public and private spheres. The inclusion of women in these structures must be decisive in reaching gender equality at many different levels. It seems logical that major decisions in the world need to be made by women and men equally. However, organs of power have been traditionally dominated by men and, to understand this discrimination, a contextualisation of the general problem of gender equality at all levels seems to be required.

Several years ago, some studies were published (Dorius and Firebaugh, 2010) which concluded that, during the last century, gender inequalities have been progressively reduced in many different fields, including economics, politics, and education. However, more recent reports, such as the World Inequality Report, stress that, far from being closer to gender equality, in the current century global inequalities have been accentuated, and women have generally been affected to a greater extent by these inequalities (Avaredo et al., 2018). In this regard, gender equality has become one of the key topics of the global humanitarian agenda in this century, and international organisations such as the United Nations consider the guarantee of a fair access for women to both education and employment a human rights question (Joshi et al., 2015). The existence of significant inequalities for women, especially those who are in emerging countries or poorer regions, in many different fields is widely known. But this problem also exists in the most developed countries. Indeed, the global index on gender equality reported by Boffey (2017) studies the situation between 2005 and 2015, and reveals the existence of important inequalities in European countries which have been hardly reduced in these last years.

In relation to the work environment, gender diversity is generally associated with the opportunities that women are provided with in the

hiring process, and in relation to their salaries and professional promotion ratings. Indeed, women remain underrepresented and continue receiving significantly lower wages than men in similar jobs, even
in developed countries, particularly at the top positions in companies
(UN Women, 2014; McKinsey Global Institute, 2018). These gaps
remain significant and persistent. For instance, in the European Union
(European Commission, 2019), women's gross hourly earnings in 2017
were on average 16.0% below those of men, although this gender pay
gap varies significantly across countries. Generally, a greater gap in salaries may be observed in the private sector, specifically in the financial
and insurance industries. In this sense, several reports have been recently
published highlighting that only a minority of the firms really incorporate gender diversity among the main priority topics of their strategic
plans and the majority of employees state that their company fails to
take effective actions to improve gender diversity.

These are really alarming data as gender equality is widely considered
to be vital to improving the sustainability of the economy and global
welfare. The situation has obviously made the interest in gender diversity
in the workplace increase exponentially and extend to different spheres.
Hence, a number of professional organisations and regulatory bodies
all over the world have considered gender diversity a business priority.
In particular, the report elaborated by the McKinsey Global Institute
(2015) shows that narrowing this gender gap in the workplace would
be positive for both ethical reasons and economic arguments, since it
would have very positive effects on the global Gross Domestic Product
(GDP) in the coming years. Therefore, these data must encourage firms
and regulators to set up policies to help close the gender gap in the
labour market.

And, what is the situation in the top decision-making structures? The
truth is that women's representation in governance structures is considerably unequal in comparison with men. Although the term governance can be explained from a different lens, a simple approach might
define governance as the exercise of political and economic authority
and decision-making in both public and private fields. All the reports
published in recent years have clearly indicated that women are still
undervalued in the workplace and are especially pushed into the background in leadership positions. Despite the global call for the inclusion of more women in governance and the progressive elimination of
the barriers for women, top positions in government and companies
continue to be occupied predominantly by men, while women feel
marginalised.

The pressures for raising female participation in governance come from many different sides and there are both supporters and detractors. Yet, what seems clear is that only gender-balanced structures could possess the ability to deal with the needs from all the population, and that fair representation in governance positions is a necessary step to realise gender diversity concerns. In the next paragraphs we first briefly talk about the outlook regarding female participation in public governments and then we focus on female representation in top business positions, especially the boards of directors, this being the book's pivotal topic.

On the one hand, there is an increasing number of international and local regulations and statements to ensure and reinforce the effective participation of women in political spheres (i.e., the 2011 United Nations General Assembly resolution on women's political participation). One of the keys to sustainable development is also the inclusion of women at the core of the political agenda and an increase in female representation in political decisions. And this moment has all the conditions to make it happen. Leaders must be therefore aware that they cannot miss the opportunity to enhance women's participation in governance mechanisms. However, although women are increasingly being politically elected, the number of women who have served as head of state or national parliamentarians is still low.

Female politicians tend to come from an elite background, from a family with political connections, or from platforms emphasising new political changes which facilitate their access to political leadership positions (Henderson and Jeydel, 2014). Nevertheless, there are still significant barriers that hinder the progression of women in political fields. In this sense, the existence of important societal and personal challenges in order to overcome some of these barriers is noteworthy. It seems clear that the cultural attitudes towards gender roles and patriarchal features of most societies hamper the access of women to politics. It is also a matter of personal pressures, as women tend to feel stronger family responsibilities and are also subject to a greater scrutiny of their private lives. Therefore, there are many pending issues and there remains a long way to go to reach equal opportunities.

On the other hand, in relation to the private sphere, women usually face important obstacles that impede their professional career in top business positions. Specifically, one of the hot topics in the political, economic, and social agenda is related to gender diversity in boards of directors, this being the most important constitution between an organisation's shareholders and management and the highest level of authority in the decision-making within a firm (Galbreath, 2018). The board of directors helps to govern firms and plays a critical role in changing the company's direction because it consists of leaders who exert considerable power over corporate strategic actions (Daily et al., 2003; Westphal and Bednar, 2005; Triana et al., 2013).

Traditionally, researchers have highlighted that the promotion of women to top decision-making positions is lessened by an invisible barrier frequently called "the glass ceiling" (Ryan et al., 2005). Although it is true that firms are making progress and reducing the gender gap in the boards of directors, much room remains for improvement, since the current figures indicate that the presence of women in the boardroom continues to be a minority. Indeed, despite the gradual increase in the number of female directors, the debate has in recent years intensified in the academic and the political sphere and has become a societal concern.

The current situation shows few women in firms' decision-making processes. Even firms have acknowledged this concern. An example is the chief executive officer (CEO) of Salesforce, Marc Benioff, who announced that the company was doing all it could to implement gender-sensitive measures and admitted that the low female participation in board meetings was worrying: "We saw in our company a lot of meetings where there were just men … I would look around the room and I'm, like, 'This meeting is just men'. Something is not right". In addition, as a response to this problem, gender diversity has been at the centre of intense policy-making, yet the effects of appointing female directors remains a controversial issue and have not been universally acknowledged (Gregory-Smith et al., 2014; Adams et al., 2015).

Although the political discussions are mainly influenced by moral reasons (promoting equality and avoiding biases and discrimination), empirical studies are increasingly encompassing economic arguments. On this subject, the academic debate about gender diversity in the board of directors has intensively increased in recent years and the related literature mainly classifies the arguments behind the promotion of women to corporate boards into two groups: the business rationale, related to economic reasons, and the social rationale, associated with moral premises (Mensi-Klarbach, 2014; Rhode and Packel, 2014; Hillman, 2015; Kumar et al., 2016).

The economic rationale to increase gender representation in boards appeals to business success as the base for corporate decision-making and advocates that board gender diversity contributes to broadening the alternatives that are considered by their members and, as a result, it may positively stimulate board members' creativity and the quality of their decisions. Therefore, according to this view, female directors are expected to add additional value due to their specific female skills and abilities, and thus improve organisational processes and performance. On the other hand, the social rationale argues that gender diversity is necessary to provide the same opportunities to groups that have been historically excluded from positions of power. The basic premise relies on the fact that women represent about half of the total population and so why do they not sit in around half of the board positions? Under this view, it could be possible to think that a mere increase in the number of female directors, if not based on economic arguments, might reduce the efficiency in decision-making processes and therefore have a negative effect on firm outcomes because women's representation prevails over the right qualification of directors. Therefore, gender diversity can also have costs, or at best, a limited effect on firm outcomes and value (Adams and Ferreira, 2009).

Regardless of the potential benefits of gender board composition for a given company, it seems evident that female participation in top business positions would bring positive social effects in terms of improving gender gaps and inequality, and positive global economic effects. However, the access of women to boards is difficult and there are important handicaps that must be coped with. First, social prejudices and patriarchal ideas in firms and society lead to creating stereotypes about the gender roles. This is a serious problem, since patriarchy is inherent not only to societies but also to individuals, and to overcome the cultural change required seems extremely complicated. Second, a number of personal issues must also be taken into consideration. Nowadays, women in top business positions still have higher visibility and their personal lives are closely examined. For example, people tend to exert greater scrutiny on the way female leaders balance their work and their family or their personal relationships.

As long as these barriers exist, the real integration of women in top business positions seems something ideal and unrealistic. In this sense, all the parts involved must understand that the selection of female directors per se is likely to be insufficient to reach an effective inclusion of women in leadership positions. Even more, regulations or fiscal incentives to increase women representation in boards may become inefficient if other additional measures are not considered. In a few words, the hiring of female board members must be accompanied by the implementation of specific and rigorous gender-related practices in order to eliminate biases and overcome the traditional stereotype that women take care rather than take charge. Accordingly, managers and executives need to be educated about the importance of minimising these biases and they should eliminate unconscious behaviours to attain a real change (Kiradjian, 2018).

In the next sections, taking into consideration the main objective of this book, we provide an overview of the current state concerning women in corporate governance structures, particularly in boards of directors. To that end, we will review the figures on female board representation and the international legislations or standards on gender diversity in boards, as well as the research on gender board composition, both from a theoretical and an empirical point of view.

2 Women in business

In order to understand the actual situation concerning female representation in corporate governance structures, specifically in boards of directors, this section carries out a short review about the limitations of
women in the workplace and serves as an introduction to comprehend
better the female contribution to the economy. Specifically, we emphasise the causes why women have found discrimination in the business
sphere, not only in companies but also in entrepreneurial activities, this
fact being related to the difficulties faced by women to reach equality in
corporate governance structures.

2.1. History of women in companies and the glass ceiling

Women have historically suffered discrimination in the workplace. In
particular, they have traditionally found significant barriers when they
attempted to reach high-level corporate positions. These historical
barriers can serve to comprehend the evolution of women in leadership
positions and their restrictions to accessing board memberships.

At the end of the nineteenth century and during the twentieth century,
mainly in the most western countries, a process to incorporate women
into professions made up until then exclusively of men was generated.
The literature on the history of professions has traditionally had an
androcentric perspective, concentrating exclusively on a masculine
vision of its evolution. Yet there is a clear gender focus in the processes
of how these professions have developed (Haynes, 2008). However, in
spite of females starting to be incorporated into companies, a characteristic of this period was the exclusion of women from institutions
that granted professional credentials – universities, colleges, or professional associations. In these places, the power of men was established
and women's access to the necessary system for their qualification or

preparation was impeded (e.g., Shackleton, 1999; Carrera et al., 2001; Jeacle, 2011; Haynes, 2017).

Meanwhile, on the world stage those years were a period of women's intense struggle: they were denied the right to vote and campaigned to get it. This suffrage movement culminated in the late nineteenth century with significant militancy and actions, which extended to the labour and professional discrimination suffered by women. At the same time, the increase of industrialisation in that period in countries such as the United Kingdom and the United States involved an important proliferation of companies. Consequently, the increase of the number of companies in developed countries brought about the demand of professionals and the first professional associations began to appear (e.g., the Institute of Accountants or the Australian Corporation of Public Accountants). Initially, as commented on above, females found many barriers to participate in these associations and obtain the certificate to practice as professionals. As a matter of fact, the most recognised economists and business leaders tended to be men. Women used to remain in the shadows in the business world, which was completely run by men. In such a scenario, it is easy to understand the unbalanced situation that still persists in corporate governance structures concerning gender equality.

Nowadays, there is a general awareness of the barriers faced by women to gain access to and be promoted in the business world, and efforts have been made from different spheres to solve this problem. But there is still a clear perception that the majority of women find invisible barriers to promotion to top corporate positions. These barriers have been extensively analysed and have generally been named "the glass ceiling", because in some ways women can see, but not reach, the top corporate hierarchy. In other words, it seems there is a transparent fence that prevents women from moving up the corporate ladder past a certain point (Morrison et al., 1987). According to this concept, Oakley (2000) argued that there are three categories that explain the barriers that women find when they attempt to get top management positions in organisations:

1. In many cases, firms develop processes of practices such as recruitment, retention, and promotion, which implicitly include any kind of discrimination of female employees. For instance, many companies fail to set up clear policies or lines of promotion that facilitate the access of women to managerial positions or board memberships.

2. Moreover, there are also cultural and behavioural causes which create stereotyping and a preferred leadership style. Regarding this, there are differences of leaderships between males and females which mean that women come across problems of tokenism, communication and leadership styles, and old boy networks. These constraints remain obvious in the business field, and investors or decision-makers in capital markets can be strongly influenced by cultural biases and stereotypes, and even consider women less competent and capable than men as leaders of companies (Carton and Rosette, 2011; Rosette et al., 2008).

3. In addition, structural and cultural reasons derived from feminist theory need to be considered. In this regard, it is widely recognised that some companies have commonly adopted a hierarchical-bureaucratic organisational model which is based on a patriarchal form of male- dominated power.

In fact, the reality confirms the existence of these barriers and all the reports show an important gender inequality in top business positions, despite the fact that nowadays there is a high female participation in line management and staff roles. A clear proof of this situation is that, currently, women make up on average 33% of junior-level staff, 24% of mid-level staff, 15% of senior-level staff and 9% of CEOs in the biggest companies in the world (World Economic Forum, 2016). Therefore, overcoming these barriers, implicit in the business world, continues to be a challenge for organisations and policy-makers.

Despite women remaining significantly underrepresented at high-level positions of companies, these restrictions are breaking down somewhat, but gender equality still seems far off. As a result, female representation in the top corporate hierarchy has progressively been considered a priority to achieve a more global gender equality objective, one that is even beneficial for firms, due to the generation of certain advantages that would improve the firm's competitiveness (Dezso and Ross, 2012).

2.2. Gender entrepreneurship

The evolution of women in business may also be understood by providing some information about the situation regarding female participation as entrepreneurs. Certainly, the role of women in the business world can also be explained by examining their influence on entrepreneurial activities. The involvement of women in entrepreneurship may be effective to reach broader objectives regarding gender equality, since it provides business activities with a female perspective. In this sense, this section establishes the main arguments for women entrepreneurship and describes the actual situation of women who decide to undertake entrepreneurship.

It is well known that entrepreneurship is key to the economy as it is an important tool in the creation of jobs, the growth of society, and innovation. To be a self-employee is an option for women in order to break down the barriers imposed by the glass ceiling (Sullivan and Meek, 2012), commented on in the previous section, and therefore join the business world. In particular, entrepreneurship contributes to the growth in women self-employees because it is associated with the equality between socioeconomic and demographic groups in society (Brush, 1992; Brush et al., 2009). Concretely, the main reasons why women pursue entrepreneurship are to a certain extent related with overcoming the barriers that prevent them from developing a full professional career in firms and reaching the top positions, and these causes can be:

- First, some women find being a self-employee an alternative to cope with the problems generally faced in firms, like unfavourable working conditions or the work-family conflict (Baron and Henry, 2011). As females often assume a higher responsibility for housework duties and childcare activities than men, women may want to become entrepreneurs if they perceive this as a solution regarding more flexible conditions (Sullivan and Meek, 2012).
- Also, frustration related to career advancement opportunities (e.g., the glass ceiling) can be determinants for women to choose to become entrepreneurs (Buttner and Moore, 1997).
- Female workers may also fail to find a comfortable relationship with their supervisors and this can generate a conflict because women consider that they might do their work better than management (Zapalska, 1997).

However, barriers against women are not exclusive to the leadership positions in firms, females have also historically found many difficulties to begin a new activity or commerce as entrepreneurs. In this regard, one of the most important handicaps for women to create a new business is related to the access to funds. Many voices have claimed that there are still important differences between females and males in the access to financial resources. In this sense, Carla Harris, chair of the National Women's Business Council (NWBC) said: "Access to capital is one of the most significant hurdles for women starting and growing their businesses". "NWBC research has shown that men tend to start their businesses with nearly twice as much financial capital than women ($135,000 versus $75,000)".

In some cases, females do not have equal access to capital because they usually have fewer financial assets and they operate in a reduced range of sectors which do not require an intensive investment. It is also common for women to lack traditional collateral (e.g., properties, often registered in men's names). In addition, females usually generate lower incomes than males and banks do not design appropriate credits adapted to women's requirements. Regardless of the reason, access to credit and capital is a significant obstacle for women in the entrepreneurship field.

But these barriers go beyond access to finance and need further analysis by all the economic agents to achieve an effective female integration in the economy. For instance, EIGE (2016) report a list of other important barriers, in addition to financial constraints, that females face when starting a business. For instance, the following handicaps are pointed out:

- Networking opportunities for women entrepreneurs. Females usually have fewer opportunities to access influential networks and they often belong to networks mostly made up of women. Meanwhile, males spend more time developing and maintaining networks (Birley et al., 1990).
- Reconciling work and family life. Traditionally, women have been recognised as having a "double burden" (work and family obligations). Accordingly, they have less available time for networking, which can lead them to experience more isolation than male entrepreneurs (Moore and Buttner, 1997). This barrier is also associated with previous arguments related to networking opportunities. At the same time, work and family tasks mean that women can spend less time on entrepreneurial activities than men.
- Prejudices and stereotypes about women in business. Entrepreneurial role models reflect a masculine bias and this is assumed by society. Thus, some studies show that females can feel out of place as a consequence of this "masculine" entrepreneurial discourse (EIGE, 2016).

Data from the European Commission reveal that in Europe women represent 52% of the total population but only 34.4% of self-employed people are women. This latter percentage has increased by around 3% from 2008 until now. Therefore, in order to promote female entrepreneurship, the European Commission has elaborated an action plan[1],

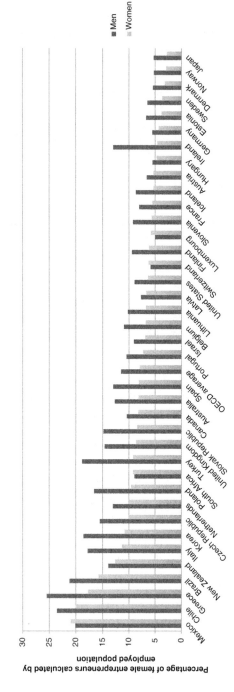

Figure 2.1 Ranking of female entrepreneurs by country for the year 2018.
Source: OECD (2019).

and one of its main initiatives is to provide support for networking among female entrepreneurs and potential female entrepreneurs.

A close look at the statistics available on female entrepreneurs shows that women prefer starting a business in certain sectors and they tend to do it on a smaller scale than men. At an international level, there are important differences between countries from the Organisation for Economic Co-operation and Development (OECD). Thus, Figure 2.1 shows the percentage of male and female self-employees by countries, sorted by the percentage of women entrepreneurs. In all the countries considered the percentage of male entrepreneurs is higher than those of females. Current figures still show that entrepreneurial activities remain controlled by men. This is a handicap for the achievement of gender equality in the business sphere.

For example, in countries such as Greece, Ireland, Italy, Korea, Poland, and Turkey, the difference between both genders is very significant. On the other hand, it is evident that there are differences between countries in women business owners. Among the countries with a lower percentage of women entrepreneurs are France, Norway, Iceland, and Sweden. This can be explained by these countries having strongly boosted the promotion of women in companies. For instance, the presence of females on the board of directors must be around 40% in some of these countries due to mandatory laws[2]. This data suggests that entrepreneurship is a mechanism for women to overcome limitations found in companies. One of the main reasons for women to become entrepreneurs is the hurdle to develop their professional career. However, in these countries there are rules to promote the access of females to top-level positions in companies and this will probably lead to higher gender equality in firms at all levels, and, therefore, they will not feel the need to start up their own businesses.

Notes

1 For more information, please visit the website: https://ec.europa.eu/growth/smes/promoting-entrepreneurship/action-plan_en.
2 The legal framework will be developed in the next section.

3 Gender board diversity

Current situation

The previous sections lead one to anticipate that gender inequalities also exist in corporate governance structures. The main objective of this book relates to gender diversity in boards of directors. In this regard, in this chapter, the international regulations regarding female participation in the boardroom are presented. These highlight the increasing attention that political and regulatory spheres pay to this topic. Moreover, a set of data is also provided so as to give a bigger picture of the evolution of women in board positions. As discussed later, the data suggests that some firms, especially in certain countries, are really making progress and implementing effective gender policies, but, at the same time, much remains to be done for improvement on an international scale.

3.1. Gender diversity in the board of directors: regulation

This section describes the existing regulations around the world concerning female representation in the boardroom. These can clearly influence the degree of participation of women in corporate governance structures. The regulations on this issue have become widespread, and originate at the beginning of the current century, when corporate governance mechanisms were strongly questioned. This was especially so after the succession of financial scandals and the recent financial crisis, which pointed to the failure of firms' governance structures and claimed for a need to improve them (Cuomo et al., 2016). As a matter of fact, in order to promote transparency and accountability, and therefore mitigate associated risks in capital markets, politicians, scholars, and the public at large have invited regulators to reinforce corporate governance rules, particularly in large firms. Specifically, the boards of directors have been at the centre of the main debates concerning the improvement of corporate governance mechanisms. As a consequence of the slow increase in the number of female directors, pointed out by many private associations (e.g., Catalyst, the EPWN), and the strong pressures from stakeholders and society in general, policy-makers continue reinforcing rules concerning female board participation. On this subject, recent regulatory reforms on board composition have become a priority in political and professional agendas and, concretely, female board representation has been one of the main focuses of these changes in corporate governance regulations. In recent years, the regulatory pressures to avoid women's underrepresentation in top-level business positions extended to an increasing number of countries (Perrault, 2015; Sila et al., 2016). Hence, different types of regulations have been adopted around the world to increase the participation of females as board members. These regulations have generally been reflected as general recommendations or as a gender-specific target or percentage, which can be included in both Codes of Corporate Governance and/or specific gender quota laws. The objective of these regulations, both codes and gender quotas, is the same: the reduction of the social and labour grievance that women have usually suffered and which has impeded them from reaching top business positions.

On the one hand, in the Codes of Corporate Governance every country can release general recommendations (without indicating concrete figures on female representation) or specific recommendations setting a target or a percentage concerning gender board diversity. These codes are a form of "flexible" regulations containing a set of voluntary governance recommendations that are considered fundamental principles related to corporate governance mechanisms in order to strengthen internal control and maximise shareholders' interests (Aguilera and Cuervo-Cazurra, 2009). These codes have increased exponentially over recent years and have been introduced in most of the developed countries. They are made up of a significant number of recommendations based on board composition. The Codes of Corporate Governance usually rely on the "comply or explain principle", which implies that companies must comply with the recommendations contained in the codes or, otherwise, explain the reasons for their unfulfillment and the selection of an alternative approach. Specifically, the board is in charge of considering each recommendation of the codes and making a decision about how the firm is going to meet with the requirements. The recommendations indicated in the codes remain voluntary and are not subject to any kind of sanction. Yet, in practice, companies tend to comply with the recommendations related to gender board diversity, at least to a certain degree, because of the negative consequences that they might suffer if they have to explain the lack of fulfilment with gender board recommendations.

In addition to these recommendations presented in the codes, many. governments have opted for specific gender laws as a more direct form of pushing firms to enhance female board representation. These impose quotas, indicating a percentage of women required in the boardroom. In theory, this kind of regulation can be expected to be more effective to force companies to increase the representation of women in corporate governance structures and reach gender quality objectives in top business positions (Labelle et al., 2015). In fact, empirical studies usually advocate that gender quotas are good policies for companies to retain, promote, and develop female talent in the board of directors (Terjesen et al., 2015). Logically, the establishment of specific gender quotas can be considered as a sort of public intervention in private decisions taken by firms and has become a controversial issue. Indeed, an intense debate has been built regarding the mixed effects that may stem from the imposition of a given percentage of women directors. Beyond the potential economic impact, the main political arguments for the existence of quotas are strictly based on fairness and equality of opportunity.

Gender quotas, which require a specific percentage of female directors, can be either voluntary or mandatory, depending on the imposition of sanctions. First, gender quotas may be considered as a voluntary law if the incompliance of these quotas does not lead to the imposition of any sanction. Sometimes, this percentage or quota is reflected as a recommended target on the Codes of Corporate Governance rather than laws of voluntary application. This model is followed by many countries (Austria, Belgium, France, Germany, Italy, the Netherlands, Norway, and Portugal). Second, gender quotas can alternatively be a mandatory law if companies are sanctioned because of their incompliance. Several countries have also adopted this system (Denmark, Finland, Greece, Slovenia, and Spain). Mandatory quotas may be classified as soft quotas and hard quotas. Soft quotas are imposed only for public companies, which can be punished due to the incompliance of the quotas. Hard quotas affect all listed companies, which are subject to sanctions in the case of incompliance. These sanctions are diverse and can range from "lax" punishments such as being excluded from public subsidies and state contracts (this happens, for example, in Spain) to obliging a firm that does not comply to de-list from a particular national stock market and/ or move the headquarters to another country (this occurs, for instance, in Norway) (Bøhren and Staubo, 2014).

To sum up, gender board composition can be regulated in several different ways. First, countries can disclose general and unspecific recommendations in the Codes of Corporate Governance to promote the access of women to the boardroom. This is the most basic form of regulation. Second, a certain percentage of female directors may be recommended, either as a desirable target in the Codes of Corporate Governance or as a quota in voluntary laws. In addition, a mandatory gender quota system, in gender laws, can also be adopted. These compulsory laws have been traditionally defined as soft quotas and hard quotas, depending on their scope of application, and the firms that are affected by the laws. In line with these criteria, the recent studies of Carrasco and Francoeur (2018) have classified the types of regulation on gender board representation into the following categories:

- Promotion of gender diversity on boards in general terms in the Codes of Corporate Governance, without indicating any specific target.
- Recommended percentage or quota of women in the board, either as a target in the Codes of Corporate Governance or a voluntary quota law. In both cases, the incompliance does not lead to the imposition of any sanction.
- Required quotas only for state-owned firms, which are sanctioned in the case of incompliance (soft quota).
- Required quotas, and associated sanctions, for all listed companies (hard quota).

In any case, nowadays, most of the developed countries have some type of regulation on gender board composition, either an unspecific recommendation or a concrete percentage of female directors. The pioneers in the disclosure of regulations on gender board diversity were Norway, Sweden, and Spain. This trend spread quickly, and immediately after these countries many others considered the need to release rules to enhance the number of female board members. The next sections present the different regulations adopted by a number of countries. For clarity, the rules implemented in each country are grouped, taking into consideration if their regulation system focuses on general recommendations on gender board diversity included in their Codes of Corporate Governance or on the establishment of a percentage of women in the board (voluntary or mandatory). To provide a picture of the situation, many examples from different countries are reported in chronological order in every section.

3.1.1. Codes of corporate governance: general recommendations on gender board diversity

This section briefly describes the general recommendations published in the Codes of Corporate Governance of several countries. In addition to these recommendations, these countries may also have a quota system, which will be commented on in the next section. In this regard, Sweden, Norway, and Spain were the first countries to include a gender recommendation in their Codes of Corporate Governance with a view to promoting the access of women to the board of directors.

Sweden, as was commented before, was one of the first countries to include a recommendation about gender diversity on boards in the Swedish Code of Corporate Governance (2004). This regulation fails to indicate a percentage or number of female directors required and just states that both genders must be represented on the board. Concretely, it establishes "the board is to have an appropriate composition, exhibiting diversity and breadth in the directors' qualifications, experience and background. An equal gender distribution on the board is to be an aim".

Norway, with the inclusion in the Norwegian Code of Practice for Corporate Governance of 2006, was also one of the first countries to consider a recommendation about gender diversity on the board of directors. Concretely, this code recommends that "the composition of the board of directors as a whole should represent sufficient diversity of background and expertise to help ensure that the board carries out its work in a satisfactory manner. In this respect due attention should be paid to the balance between male and female members of the board".

Spain, in the Unified Code of Corporate Governance, which was published in 2006, included a recommendation regarding gender diversity on boards. Specifically, the 14th recommendation of the Code established that "when women directors are few or non-existent, the board should state the reasons for this situation and the measures taken to correct it; in particular, the Nomination Committee should take steps to ensure that:

a) The process of filling board vacancies has no implicit bias against women candidates;
b) The company makes a conscious effort to include women within the target of the candidates for board places".

These actions had a great deal of societal repercussions that extended to the international political field and, as a result, similar rules were rapidly adopted by other countries (Italy, Japan, the United Kingdom, the United States, among others) that also disclosed recommendations about gender board diversity. Some of these recommendations are briefly commented on below.

Belgium, in its Code of Corporate Governance published in 2009, considered a recommendation regarding gender diversity on the board.

In particular, this established that "the board's composition should ensure that decisions are made in the corporate interest. It should be determined on the basis of gender diversity and diversity in general, as well as complementary skills, experience and knowledge".

The Finnish Corporate Governance Code 2010 introduced, as part of the reform of the Corporate Governance Code, a new recommendation concerning the principles related to diversity on the board of directors. The new recommendation establishes: "One element of a diverse composition of the board is to have both genders represented on the board".

The United Kingdom Corporate Governance Code from 2012 also considered that "the search for board candidates should be conducted, and appointments made, on merit, against objective criteria and with due regard for the benefits of diversity on the board, including gender". This criterion has also been adopted in the United Kingdom Corporate Governance Code since 2016.

In the same sense, the Code of Corporate Governance published in Denmark in 2014 also included a recommendation on gender board representation. Concretely, "the selection and nomination of candidates for the board of directors must be carried out through a thoroughly transparent process approved by the board of directors overall. When assessing its composition and nominating new candidates, the board of directors must take into consideration the need for the integration of new talent and diversity in relation to age, international experience and gender".

In addition, the Italian Stewardship Principles, from 2014, included a reference to gender diversity. Concretely, when talking about the selection of board members, this document says "in carrying out such an assessment, it is required to verify that, according to the issuer's business, the various members (executive, non-executive, independent) and the professional and managerial competences, including international experience, are adequately represented, taking into account also the benefits that could stem from the presence of different genders, age and seniority".

The Japanese Corporate Governance Code from 2014 recommended that "companies should recognise that the existence of diverse perspectives and values reflecting a variety of experiences, skills and characteristics is a strength that supports their sustainable growth. As such, companies should promote a diversity of personnel, including the active participation of women".

In line with the previous codes, the Ontario Securities Commission introduced in the Corporate Governance Code in 2015 for Canadian listed companies a requirement for companies listed on the Toronto Stock Exchange to disclose annually how many women are on their board and in executive officer positions. It also compels disclosure on related aspects including whether the company has a policy for identifying and nominating female directors, and whether there are targets at either the board or executive level, and if not to explain why.

The United States also released gender board recommendations. These were published in the year 2016 in the Principles of Corporate Governance, considering that "diverse backgrounds and experiences on corporate boards, including those of directors who represent the broad range of society, strengthen board performance and promote the creation of long-term shareholder value. Boards should develop a framework for identifying appropriately diverse candidates that allows the nominating/corporate governance committee to consider women, minorities and others with diverse backgrounds as candidates for each open board seat".

More recently, the current French Code of Corporate Governance elaborated in 2018 also presents a gender board recommendation in general terms: "Each Board should consider what the desirable balance of its membership and that of the Board committees should be, particularly in terms of diversity (gender representation, nationalities, age, qualifications, professional experience, etc.)".

3.1.2. *Specific targets on female board representation*

This section focuses on the countries that have established a percentage or quota of women in the board for their companies, regardless of this percentage being a recommendation in the Codes of Corporate Governance, appearing in a voluntary law, or in a mandatory law.

The first country to impose a required percentage of female directors was Norway, with the introduction of a mandatory gender quota of 40% for the boards of all public limited companies. Particularly, the Norwegian Code of Practice for Corporate Governance of 2007 also considered that the composition of the board of directors related to the gender of its members had to satisfy the requirements of the Norwegian Public Limited Liability Companies Act. This law required that the boards of publicly listed companies had at least 40% female representation in 2008.

Spain was the second country in the world to pass a gender quota law (the so-called "Law of Equality" enacted in 2007). This promotes women as boardroom members. The objective of this law, which had no associated sanctions, was to attain 40% of women on the boards of directors by 2015 (in the year before the implementation of this compulsory legislation, 2006, this percentage was only 3.5%). In addition, the Spanish Good Governance Code of Listed Companies, published in the year 2015 recommended that "the director selection policy should pursue the goal of having at least 30% of total board places occupied by women directors before the year 2020". It is important to mention that Spain has approved a law (Real Decreto-ley 6/2019, March 1) to modify the previous Law of Equality enacted in 2007. The aim of this new rule is to be more restrictive with gender diversity in companies. Concretely, it establishes a three-year term for companies with more than 50 workers to develop and apply an equality plan, two years for those from 100 to 150 and one year for those from 150 to 250. Until now it was only mandatory for companies with more than 250 workers.

Iceland, following the Norwegian example was, in 2010, the third country to impose mandatory quotas. It was specifically required that companies with over 50 employees on a yearly basis had at least 40% of each gender represented on their corporate boards of directors from September 2013.

On the other hand, in 2010, France included a quota in its Code of Corporate Governance for the first time. Concretely, it was established that "in order to reach such a balance, the objective is that each board shall reach and maintain a percentage of at least 20% of women within a period of three years and at least 40% of women within a period of six years, from the date of publication of this recommendation or from the date of the listing of the company's shares on a regulated market, whichever is later". Moreover, "when the board is comprised of fewer than 9 members, the gap at the end of six years, between the number of directors of each gender, may not be in excess of two". The main objective of this recommendation was that all boards should realise and then maintain a percentage of at least 40% women as of the shareholders' meeting of 2016. This quota was later reflected in a mandatory law in 2014 (Law 2014–873, August 4, 2014), with sanctions for its incompliance. After this mandatory regulation, the new French Code of Corporate Governance changed and currently only a general recommendation appears[1].

On the other hand, in the United Kingdom the approach to gender diversity on boards has been less strict. Thus, the Davies Report (2011), which is the code of corporate governance for the United Kingdom regarding gender diversity on boards, focused its attention on the paucity of female directors and included a recommendation that 25% of directors of the board should be women by 2015 and the condition that if this recommendation was not complied with by companies a quota system would be imposed. However, when amended in 2012, the United Kingdom Corporate Governance Code did not include this target, only requiring listed companies to establish a policy concerning boardroom diversity, including measurable objectives for implementing the policy.

On 14 November 2012 the European Commission published a Directive with the purpose of fighting against the discrimination experienced by women in the top positions in Europe's biggest companies. This Directive proposed legislation with the "objective of a 40% presence of the under-represented sex among the non-executive directors of companies listed on stock exchanges and by requiring companies with a lower share of the under-represented sex among the non-executive directors to introduce pre-established, clear, neutrally formulated and unambiguous criteria in selection procedures for those positions in order to attain that objective" (European Commission, 2012). Regarding the time that companies had to take into consideration this Directive, it was established that "the Commission shall then issue a specific report ascertaining whether those measures effectively enable members of the under-represented sex to hold at least 40 per cent of the non-executive director positions by 1 January 2018 for listed companies which are public undertakings, and by 1 January 2020 for listed companies which are not public undertakings" (European Commission, 2012). Therefore, in the European Union context some countries have introduced measures on either a voluntary or a mandatory basis.

For instance, in the German Corporate Governance Code it has been included since 2017 that "in listed corporations subject to the Co-determination Act, the Co-determination Act for the Coal, Iron and Steel Industry or the Act Supplementing the Co-determination Act for the Coal, Iron and Steel Industry, the Supervisory Board comprises at least 30% women and at least 30% men. In other corporations subject to the Gender Equality Act, the Supervisory Board determines targets for the share of female members. With effect from 1 January 2016, the minimum share of 30%, respectively, for men and women members of the Supervisory Board must be observed in any new elections or delegations that become necessary for filling individual or several positions on a Supervisory Board (Law on Equal Participation of Men and Women in Private-Sector and Public-Sector Management Positions, Section 25 Subsection 1 EG-AktG (Introductory Law of the German Stock Corporation Act), German Federal Gazette I. 2015, 642, 656[2])".

Other countries belonging to the European Union, such as Austria, Belgium, Italy, the Netherlands, and Portugal, now have mandatory quotas ranging from 30 to 40% of female board membership, while Denmark, Finland, Greece, and Slovenia have voluntary quotas. Austria

(Law on Equality for Women and Men as Non-Executive Directors on Company Boards, implemented from 1 January 2018) and Portugal (Law 62/2017, 1 August) have been the last countries to impose mandatory gender quotas.

Therefore, the establishment of quotas seems to be a trend. Apart from the European Union, other influential countries (Australia, Brazil, Chile) have considered the need for a minimum representation of women in the boards of directors, and gender quotas are under discussion by the governments.

3.2. Gender diversity in the board of directors: the current situation

As a response to the increasing regulations on gender board composition and the societal concern about gender equality at all levels, including top business positions, the number of women in leadership posts has increased in the majority of the countries. In fact, the current statistics confirm the enhancement in female board participation but, at the same time, underline that gender parity remains an important challenge. Indeed, female board representation fails to reach the required figures in many countries. In this section, an overview of the actual situation is provided. First, information concerning the presence of women in the boardroom is reported. Second, and more specifically, data about women who hold the most powerful position in the board, the CEO, is also presented.

3.2.1. Women in the boardroom

Table 3.1 shows the proportion of female directors for a significant number of countries, together with the associated gender regulation in relation to female board representation. We note that women still remain underrepresented in the board of directors, the proportion of women in the boardroom being scarce in many countries. Yet, European Union countries seem to have started to overcome handicaps for women to access leadership positions and the number of female directors in European countries tends to be greater than elsewhere.

A detailed look at the data reveals that there is a group of countries where female board representation exceeds or stays very close to the established requirements. Thus, Norway, which has traditionally been considered a pioneer in the fight against women discrimination in leadership positions (Carrasco and Laffarga, 2006), almost reaches gender

Table 3.1 Proportion of women directors on the board and gender quota by country.

Country	% of women directors represented on the board	Gender quota and expected date	Code of regulation	Type of regulation
Austria	19.2%	30% in 2018	4	Hard quota
Belgium	32.1%	33% in 2017	4	Hard quota
Canada	27%	No gender quota	2	Voluntary target
China	9.8%	No gender quota	0	None
Denmark	27.6%	30% in 2013	2	Voluntary target
Finland	33.3%	No gender quota	3	Soft quota
France	42.5%	40% in 2017	4	Hard quota
Germany	32%	40% in 2016	4	Hard quota
Greece	11.3%	No gender quota	3	Soft quota
Iceland	45.2%	40% in 2013	4	Hard quota
India	12.3%	At least one woman in the year 2015	4	Hard quota
Italy	32.3%	33% in 2016	4	Hard quota
Japan	6.5%	30% in 2020	2	Voluntary target
Kenya	19.8%	33%*	3	Soft quota
Netherlands	21.6%	30% in 2015	2	Voluntary target
Nigeria	11.5%	No gender quota	2	Voluntary target
Norway	45.6%	40% in 2008	4	Hard quota
Portugal	16.2%	33.3% in 2020	4	Hard quota
Russia	7.8%	No gender quota	0	None
South Africa	17.4%	No gender quota	1	General recommendation
Spain	19.5%	40% in 2015	2	Voluntary target
Sweden	39.1%	No gender quota	1	General recommendation
Switzerland	24%	No gender quota	1	General recommendation
Slovenia	22.6%	No gender quota	1	General recommendation
United Kingdom	27.5%	25% in 2015	2	Voluntary target
United States	24%	No gender quota	1	General recommendation

* This percentage has been considered because the Kenyan constitution requires that "of the elective or appointive bodies of a company, no more than two-thirds of the members be of the same gender".
Source: Carrasco and Francoeur (2018), Fraser-Moleketi and Mizrahi (2015), Spencer Stuart (2018), European Commission (2018).

parity in the boardroom. The proportion of female directors in firms from Iceland and France also exceeds that needed. These high levels of gender representation may be explained due to the existence of hard quotas in all these countries, requiring at least 40% of female directors (in 2008 for Norway, 2013 for Iceland, and 2017 for France). Sweden, which has also been one of the first countries to promote gender board diversity, also presents a high female representation in the boardroom, irrespective of the existence of a particular quota.

Another group consists of those countries whose firms have boards composed of about one third women, such as Belgium, Finland, Germany, and Italy. This confirms the decisions that have been taken by European firms to really include gender board diversity in their agenda. This progress has possibly been made as a consequence of legal regulations or other measures in order to encourage gender board balance as a commitment to gender equality objectives (European Commission, 2018).

The proportion of female board members in other countries, such as Denmark and the United Kingdom, is about 27%, similar to the percentage required, 30% and 25%, respectively. Female board representation remains around 25% in Canada and the United States, regardless of the lack of any specific target or quota.

More surprising is the case of Spain, which released general recommendations on gender board diversity and even established quotas many years ago, yet the percentage of female directors is under 20%. The data also indicates that the proportion of women in the boardroom in firms from Austria, Japan, the Netherlands, and Portugal is still far from the target required. The situation in Japan is especially worrying. Here female directors represent only 6.5% of board members. Other countries with an alarming scenario are China and Russia, since the proportion of women in their boards fails to reach 10%.

In order to provide more information about the situation of every country, Table 3.1 also includes data about the existing regulation, grouping the different systems according to the classifications provided by the relevant previous literature. In this sense, prior research made a differentiation between countries without rules, countries with voluntary rules, and countries with mandatory rules (Terjesen et al., 2015; Terjesen and Sealy, 2016; Carrasco and Francoeur, 2018). Consistent with this approach, five different groups are identified in that table in the columns "code of regulation" and "type of regulation". These groups, classified in the categories presented in the previous section, are: (0) Countries without any regulation or recommendation related to gender diversity on boards; (1) Countries that promote gender diversity on boards without a specific target (general recommendation); (2) Countries that have established a specific recommended percentage, either a target in the codes or a voluntary quota law but do not impose any sanction in the case of non-compliance with the regulation or recommendation (voluntary target); (3) Countries that have imposed quotas or targets exclusively for state-owned firms, which are subject to sanctions in the event of incompliance (soft quota); (4) Countries that have imposed quotas for all listed companies and impose sanctions in the case of incompliance (hard quota).

This data can be complemented with those provided in Figure 3.1, which reports information on the evolution of gender diversity on boards by European countries during the period 2003–2018. In general, the presence of women in the boardroom has been enhanced in the vast majority of countries. Specifically, the data confirms that European countries, probably pushed by the increased regulation on gender board representation (through the establishment of quotas), have dramatically increased the number of women in the board of directors. The evolution shown in Iceland, France, and Italy in order to reach the requirements concerning female board participation is particularly remarkable. On the other hand, Norway represents an interesting case, since the female board representation has increased by only 19% in the last 15 years. This can be explained by this country having been a pioneer in the promotion of women directors on boards and, consequently, female board participation has remained high in recent years.

Although most of the countries have made significant efforts to increase the presence of women in boards, there is a group of countries with much room for improvement. Thus, for example, Figure 3.1 indicates that in some regions such as Turkey, Serbia, Slovenia, Cyprus, Montenegro, Croatia, the Czech Republic, Bulgaria, and Greece, the increase in female board representation is very low. In some countries (e.g., Lithuania, Estonia, and Romania), the presence of women in the board of directors has even decreased during the period 2003–2018. This can be a direct consequence of the lack of any quotas or recommendations related to gender diversity on boards in these countries.

To sum up, taking into consideration the information from Table 3.1 and Figure 3.1, it can be highlighted that although female underrepresentation in the boards seems a general norm, some countries have made significant efforts towards gender board balance. The countries with higher levels of female board representation tend to be European, especially those that have specific regulations on gender board diversity based either on quotas or on recommendations. On the other

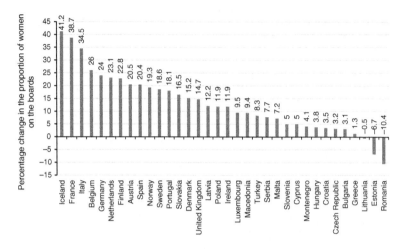

Figure 3.1 Evolution of gender diversity on boards by country during the period 2003–2018.

Source: European Institute for Gender Equality, Gender Statistics Database.

hand, eastern European countries generally present an alarming scenario, characterised by the lack of gender regulations and the need to create a greater awareness concerning gender policies. In other words, the national cultural environment and policies adopted by governments shape women's participation in corporate structures (World Economic Forum, 2016).

In addition to the national divergences, female board representation may also differ depending on the industry in which firms operate. In this sense, recent statistics (Data Morphosis, 2019) indicate that the presence of women in the boardroom varies across industries, thus suggesting the existence of particular barriers associated with the sector of activity. A summary of these statistics is shown in Table 3.2, which reports information about gender board diversity by industry and regions. Thus, it is possible to distinguish sectors where the presence of women on boards has traditionally been scarce, such as "Basic materials", "Oil and gas", and "Financials".

Regarding the effect of the industry on the number of women in a board, some authors affirm that the sector which a company belongs to conditions the promotion of female directors (Harrigan, 1981; Fryxell and Lerner, 1989; Bertrand and Hallock, 2000). Thus, females usually participate more in service-oriented, labour-intensive, or women's products industries than in manufacturing (Harrigan, 1981). Women

Table 3.2 Percentage of women directors by sectors and regions.

Sector	Europe	Africa	Asia Pacific	Latin America	Middle East	North America	Mean percentage of women
Basic materials	9.7%	15.6%	6.2%	4.0%	15.9%	7.7%	9.9%
Consumer goods	16.0%	16.6%	9.4%	6.3%	11.7%	13.7%	12.3%
Consumer services	16.2%	17.6%	11.7%	8.6%	4.0%	13.7%	12.0%
Financials	13.9%	17.2%	9.9%	4.8%	7.0%	12.4%	10.9%
Health care	13.9%	17.1%	11.1%	0.0%	15.7%	9.9%	11.3%
Industrials	14.0%	15.6%	7.4%	5.8%	14.4%	9.7%	11.2%
Oil and gas	11.2%	16.2%	6.5%	6.4%	13.9%	6.0%	10.0%
Technology	12.6%	23.0%	6.3%	25.0%	19.3%	7.0%	15.5%
Telecommunications	14.5%	13.0%	9.1%	6.3%	13.1%	8.6%	10.8%
Utilities	14.4%	53.8%	7.0%	6.4%	21.6%	17.8%	20.2%

Source: Data Morphosis (2019).

are more prevalent in companies that are specialised in healthcare and social industries and in trade sectors (Bertrand and Hallock, 2000). They do not usually belong to less innovative sectors, and industries such as the retail, science, technology, and engineering sectors, which are mostly dominated by men (EIGE, 2016). However, the data reported in Table 3.2 fails to be totally consistent with these arguments, probably due to the bias that may be derived from the sample design.

As to the distribution by regions, the high representation of women for all sectors in Africa is very relevant. These results are in line with findings from Carrasco and Francouer (2018). Meanwhile, in an opposite position is the Latin America region, where the presence of female directors is very scarce for all sectors except in the technology sector.

In general, all the data reported confirm the underrepresentation of women in boards, despite the increased legal efforts. In practice, in addition to the regulations and industry contexts, there are some circumstances that condition female board representation. The previous literature analysing the factors that determine women's promotion to boards of directors usually identifies the following: cultural environment (Adams and Kirchmaier, 2015; Carrasco et al., 2015), personal characteristics of directors (Singh and Vinnicombe, 2004; Sheridan and Milgate, 2005), and board structure and/or composition (Westphal and Zajac, 1995; Westphal and Milton, 2000; Westphal and Stern, 2007; Bravo and Reguera-Alvarado, 2019). One line of research that is receiving great attention and can be a determinant of the presence of females in boards of directors is related to the cultural factors of the countries. This is because researchers have demonstrated that the national culture is the most important characteristic associated with board gender diversity (Grosvold and Brammer, 2011; Adams and Kirchmaier, 2015; Carrasco et al., 2015). A country's culture determines the set of beliefs and values that are shared by their citizens (Hofstede, 1980). In this sense, the very concept of gender is a cultural construct which has been brought about to be applied to differences between men and women in society with respect to attitude, mental structures, and expectations (Carrasco et al., 2015). Therefore, social beliefs concerning the roles of men and women mean generating notions such as gender equality or discrimination. Authors who have studied the link between gender diversity and cultural factors have found that the work done by politicians and regulators is very important because they can determine the role of women in society and, particularly, their access to posts of responsibility which have been traditionally reserved for men (Carrasco et al., 2015). Meanwhile, Terjesen et al. (2015) affirm that countries which introduce greater family policies, especially those related to maternity benefits, are aligned with egalitarian values in terms of gender and, given these national cultural aspects and societal values, have more affinity in promoting gender diversity on boards and impose laws to get gender quotas. By contrast, there are few possibilities of those countries with soft family policies developing and enacting gender quota policies. Following these arguments, Inglehart and Norris (2003) concluded that Finland, Sweden, Germany, Canada, and Norway are the countries more committed to gender equality. Nigeria, Morocco, Egypt, Bangladesh, and Jordan, for example, are to be found in the opposite situation.

The link between gender diversity on boards and the cultural framework is supported by institutional theory[3] because a country's culture is intimately related to its institutional environment. This theory is based on the beliefs that the institutional environment conditions companies and the institutional rules present in a particular society are key to its corporate models (Meyer and Rowan, 1977). Based on this theory, Hofstede (1980) concludes that cultural differences explain why countries give a different answer to a similar social phenomenon. Therefore, this background explains differences between countries related to the incorporation of females into firms and the imposition of a legal framework to facilitate the access of women to high-level positions in companies.

Other factors that may determine the presence of women in the boardroom are those associated with their personal characteristics, such as their experience, skills, and knowledge, related to their human capital accumulated over time (Becker, 1993). In addition, social networks, in other words, social capital, is also another essential characteristic to explain the presence of women in boards of directors (Portes, 1998). The underrepresentation of women in boards can be therefore partially explained by them having been traditionally excluded from top business positions, hence resulting in men generally having superior experience and skills in leadership posts, and greater social networks. As a result, the lack of these features can sometimes explain the low presence of female directors (Singh and Vinnicombe, 2004).

Meanwhile, concerning board characteristics, the existence of gender diversity in governance structures and the board of directors in particular is very relevant at the moment of the selection of board members. In this sense, the literature sustains that there is a gender effect in director selection, which means that the likelihood of incorporating a female director into a board depends on the number of women currently belonging to it and the desertion of female directors from the board. For instance, the exit of a woman from the board of directors is likely to increase the probability of a new woman being added to the board (Farrell and Hersch, 2005).

3.2.2. Women as chief executive officers

One decisive instrument in the reduction or banishing of the traditional barriers associated with the promotion of women in the workplace is linked to the presence of women in very high leadership positions, and having a strong visible power and legitimacy (Bilimoria, 2006). In this sense, firms with women in key strategic decision-making positions and extremely powerful posts are likely to send a crucial message to society regarding their commitment to the progress of women at all levels to achieve gender equality (Daily and Dalton, 2003). As to the corporate governance structures and specifically the board of directors, the most representative and powerful post remains the CEO. In line with the previous argument, it can be assumed that firms with women CEOs are in an excellent position to reach gender diversity objectives in governance structures. Accordingly, Christy Glass, a professor at Utah State University, considers that "when women lead companies at the board rank and as CEOs, (there's) more attention (paid) to equality policies and practices".

Nevertheless, reality shows that the access to CEO positions remains very difficult for women. The inclusion of female directors to the board has progressively increased, possibly because of the enhanced regulatory and societal pressures, but women still find significant barriers when they attempt to move to the highest and most powerful positions in companies, thus suggesting the existence of a kind of glass ceiling. Codes of Corporate Governance and legislations generally promote gender diversity in the boardroom in terms of representation rather than participation in key positions. As a matter of fact, the female representation in boards as CEOs is low in most of the countries, as shown in Figure 3.2. This is commented on in more detail later. Other data that maintain this gender gap in the most powerful governance structures can be associated with the time that women and men take to reach CEO posts. Regarding this, a good example is the mean age of the 50 first female CEOs that lead Fortune 500 companies, which is around 50 years old. Their range of age is from 46 to 68 years old. The data indicates that women do not usually get high-level positions as young as men. Moreover, in the rankings related to the most important or relevant

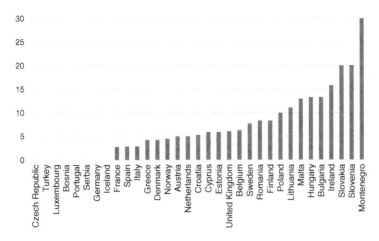

Figure 3.2 Proportion of women CEOs on the board of directors in 2018.
Source: European Institute for Gender Equality, Gender Statistics Database.

CEOs in companies elaborated by representative organisations around the world, such as Bloomberg or Forbes, there are not any women among the first positions. This data is to be expected, taking into consideration that, of the 500 companies that make up the Fortune 500, just 24 firms had a woman CEO during the year 2018, representing 4.8%.

Traditionally, women come across many difficulties in reaching the most powerful posts in firms, and female CEOs are extremely rare in large corporations. This can be observed in Figure 3.2, which shows the proportion of women CEOs on the board of directors for 2018 in a sample of 33 European countries. It can be seen that, despite the regulatory efforts and the implementation of a legal framework in some countries, female board representation in CEO positions currently remains scarce, although there are substantial differences depending on the country. It is true that the legal system can promote the presence of women on the board of directors. However, despite the increasing legal reforms, the percentage of female CEOs remains very low. Concretely, in some countries there is not any woman who occupies this position on the board. For example, this takes place in countries such as the Czech Republic, Turkey, Luxembourg, Bosnia and Herzegovina, Portugal, Serbia, Germany, and Iceland. A surprising data is that Norway, which has traditionally been a pioneer country in promoting the presence of women on boards and in complying with gender quotas, presents a low percentage of women CEOs (4.5%), and as a result is not one of the countries with a higher percentage of female CEOs.

In relation to these data, Fortune 500 has elaborated a ranking of the "most powerful women" in business where four criteria are considered: the size and importance of the woman's business in the global economy, the health and direction of the business, the arc of the woman's career, and social and cultural influence. In line with the data from Figure 3.2, the study developed by Fortune 500 for the year 2018 shows that the proportion of women CEOs continues to be scarce. The number of female CEOs in the Fortune 500 has even gone down from 32 to 24 in that year, therefore the momentum can stall. In other words, although increases in gender diversity can be a first step, female participation in boards can become symbolic and is far from the most powerful positions. As Stacey Abrams, the Democratic nominee for Governor of Georgia, said, "We can toast achievement, but we must continue to demand more, to demand parity", and this should be extensive in all levels. Actual gender equality in boards of directors would be achieved not only by reaching gender parity in terms of representation but also by including female directors in key decision-making positions.

Notes

1 In the previous Section 2.3.1, the recommendation related to gender diversity included in the current Code of Corporate Governance of France from the year 2018 has been commented on.
2 This is the code of corporate governance from Germany published in 2015.
3 This theory is described in the next section of this book.

4 Women's contribution to boards
A theoretical approach

As commented on in the previous chapter, there is a growing consensus about the importance of gender diversity in the top positions of firms, but the benefits of having more women in high-level decision-making structures remains an open question and two opposing views are generally identified. The first highlights that women make a positive contribution to the boardroom. The second argues that female directors may harm the functioning of boards. Specifically, this chapter focuses, from a theoretical perspective, on the expected contribution of female directors to the boardroom and, consequently, on the potential impact of female directors on firm outcomes. This section can be useful for academics, firms, and policy-makers to have a better picture of the arguments that may explain the influence of women in boards of directors.

As a previous step, we briefly describe the role of boards of directors as a corporate governance mechanism. Then, the main theoretical approaches used by researchers to explain the possible effect of gender board composition are summarised.

Corporate governance has been traditionally defined as a group of rules and practices by which a company is directed and controlled in order to mitigate conflicts of interest between managers and shareholders (Shleifer and Vishny, 1997). In particular, the board of directors has commonly been considered to be the core of corporate governance structures. The board of directors is the top-level decision-making system of organisations, and has the authority to hire, fire, and compensate the managers and to ratify and monitor important corporate strategies (Fama and Jensen, 1983). Boards serve critical functions in firms in formulating and implementing strategy and provide important benefits to a firm such as advice and counsel, connections to environmental contingencies, and legitimacy (Hillman and Dalziel, 2003). Specifically, boards are in charge of a number of tasks related to the governing of a firm and therefore they must establish global policies and objectives, assess the performance of CEOs, control the accessibility of financial resources, approve annual budgets, and set the compensation systems of management, among other functions (McNamara, 2001). A key job of the boards is to delegate responsibilities to ensure that the management does not deviate from those recommendations that have been implemented by the board in order to protect the interests of the shareholders (Detthamrong et al., 2017). To that end, several board subcommittees are designed for the monitoring of these specific tasks. These committees usually receive names such as the nomination committee, the compensation committee, the audit committee, or the corporate governance committee. The literature on boards of directors is characterised by theoretical pluralism and, subsequently, there are different theories from various disciplines to explain the roles of boards (Madhani, 2017).

In particular, research on boards of directors has considerably increased in the last decades, especially because recent scandals have evidenced that failures in boards may be extremely harmful for the global economy and society (Rhodel and Packel, 2014). Therefore, the composition and functioning of the board of directors is under strong scrutiny, especially after the globalisation of capital markets and the succession of financial scandals. These have stressed the need to improve corporate governance mechanisms (Pugliese et al., 2009).

Habitually, researchers have focused on board composition to examine the dynamics and influence of boards of directors. In this regard, studies have largely analysed characteristics such as board independence or board size. However, more recently, other board attributes have attracted great interest (Johnson et al., 2013). For example, a growing body of research has considered human and social capital characteristics as relevant features to understand the decision-making process within a board, including different measures related to specific kinds of expertise, experience, tenure, social status, or links to other companies. In addition, demographic attributes of directors, such as age, education, gender, and ethnicity, have also attracted the attention of scholars. Concretely, many studies have advocated that these demographic characteristics of directors (Joshi et al., 2011) are crucial to understand how boards behave, make decisions, and consequently affect firm outcomes. Despite the increased research on board composition, there is still relatively little consensus about what kinds of people make the best board members (Johnson et al., 2013). On the one hand, any single theory cannot fully explain the potential effect of boards on firm outcomes. On the other hand, the empirical evidence is also inconclusive.

Among these characteristics analysed, gender diversity has undoubtedly generated a huge debate with reference to its impact on boardroom dynamics (Dawar and Singh, 2016; Abad et al., 2017). In line with this, a growing branch of research has searched for evidence about the actual effects of director gender, under the assumption that gender diversity affects board skills, dynamics, and decision-making and, as a result, firm-level outcomes, but the empirical findings are still far from definitive. In this section, a summary of the main theoretical arguments concerning the potential effects of gender diversity in boards is described. Since this topic is obviously multidisciplinary, a single theoretical argument cannot provide a complete framework to explain the association between gender board diversity and corporate decisions (Pugliese et al., 2009). The majority of these theoretical approaches support a positive effect of gender board composition on firm-level outcomes, yet researchers also provide arguments to justify the existence of negative effects derived from gender diversity in boards.

The idea that the gender composition can make a difference to how individuals within the group act and make decisions is old, and the literature has commonly employed two major and contradictory views:

- First, studies often employ economic arguments to justify that gender diversity in the boardroom is a business case that improves economic outcomes. In line with this perspective, we can select from several theories among the ones most commonly used by researchers all around the world, each of which considers different perspectives that might serve to explain the contributions of female directors. These theories are generally based on certain gendered presumptions and assume that women possess different skills to men, which can add value to the boards of directors. In particular, the well-known agency theory has dominated this type of research, although other theoretical approaches can provide interesting insights (García-Meca and Palacios, 2018). In this theoretical review, the following theories will be briefly explained: agency theory, stakeholder theory, psychological theories, resource dependence theory, institutional theory, stewardship theory, and signalling theory.
- Second, a few studies have employed the opposite rationale. They state that gender diversity could have negative consequences in firm-level outcomes if women have been appointed for social or moral reasons. From a theoretical approach, these negative effects are explained through several arguments, highlighting those used

from a tokenism perspective and those extracted from a group phenomena perspective. Both arguments are also discussed below.

It is worth mentioning that all the arguments commented on are
presented below as complementary theoretical approaches. Actually
some of the ideas of these theories might be similar or overlapping in
some cases. It is also important to clarify that the order of presentation
does not indicate any prevalence or priority.

4.1. Agency theory

Agency theory was the earliest fully developed theory in the corporate
governance field and has been predominant in the studies about boards
of directors. This theory relies on the premise that shareholders and
managers have different interests and so the way in which both groups
of agents act is characterised by self-centred opportunism (Jensen and
Meckling, 1976). In the current globalised context, the great separation of ownership and control in most large organisations is expected
to cause significant divergences and conflicts of interest between managers (often called agents) and shareholders (who are frequently named
principals). This conflict of interest has become a crucial matter in board
research. In addition, most of the regulations and recommendations
consider that the main objective of corporate governance structures,
including boards, should play an important role in the mitigation of
these conflicts, thereby monitoring and controlling the decisions made
by the managers in order to protect the interests of shareholders (Fama
and Jensen, 1983).

In particular, gender diversity has been more recently integrated into
the theoretical framework extracted from agency theory, as researchers
have documented that the presence of female directors improves the
ability of boards to supervise management (Francoeur et al., 2008).
Several arguments have been provided in order to explain why gender
diversity can improve a board's effectiveness and its critical function of
reducing agency conflicts, although most of these explanations agree
that women tend to enhance the degree of board independence (Carter
et al., 2003; Adams and Ferreira, 2009; Terjesen and Sealy, 2016). In
theory, the neutral selection of board members, avoiding gender bias
practices, should optimise independence. In other words, boards with
a greater gender representation are more heterogeneous, which would
mean that the directors would be subject to fewer external influences
(Cabrera et al., 2016). On this subject, boards with more women
would tend to be more active and more prone to ask questions that

traditionally might not be asked by men, and therefore an increase in the proportion of female directors is likely to drive greater insight and closer monitoring. To sum up, under an agency view, female directors may bring benefits to a firm because they can make the board more independent to take actions to restrain managers from adopting an opportunistic behaviour. This will safeguard the interests of shareholders.

4.2. Stakeholder theory

Stakeholder theory is also a well-known theory in business and management studies, and it focuses on values in managing an organisation (Freeman et al., 2010). Stakeholders are broadly defined as all those whose participation is critical to the survival of the organisation, including managers, employees, customers, suppliers, consumers, regulators, government, media, and local communities. Supporters of this theory suggest that the long-term survival of a company is dependent on the commitment of all these stakeholders and not only the shareholders. As to the corporate governance area, and in line with the previous idea, the main premise of stakeholder theory assumes that board members need to recognise and consider the different interests that come from all a firm's various stakeholders. In other words, the inclusion of diverse directors should help to broaden the representation of a wider range of societal opinions, to empathise with all the stakeholders and to avoid the supremacy that one group with particular interests might have (Chambers et al., 2013).

Therefore, it is easy to understand that this theory has also been widely used in the analysis of the phenomenon of gender diversity in the boardroom, particularly because the inclusion of female directors is likely to change the stakeholder's orientation of the firm (Oakley, 2000). On the one hand, the participation of women on boards is perceived per se to be a good policy for a company. Indeed, companies that incorporate female directors can better accomplish stakeholders' expectations and thus serve their demands (Dallas, 2002). On the other hand, female board members are more oriented to the different stakeholders' concerns. Compared with men, women have a different perception concerning leadership roles (Wood and Eagly, 2009). In particular, female directors have a more communal style of leadership and as a result, boards with a greater gender diversity are more likely to focus on issues and policies concerning the welfare of other people (Tejedo-Romero et al., 2017) and to implement more open government processes and the incorporation of stakeholders' interests (Hillman et al., 2002). The previous literature has commonly indicated that women have strong communal characteristics because they tend to be more supportive, empathic, interpersonally sensitive, and gentle (Nielsen and Huse, 2010). As a consequence, female directors are expected to push the board to be more socially sensitive and to pay particular attention to different stakeholders' concerns. This may be translated into more positive firm-level outcomes (Liao et al., 2015). Moreover, another notion derived from stakeholder theory is the idea that a more gender-diverse board is in a better position to understand the reality of the markets that the company targets by identifying the main stakeholders' demands (Oakley, 2000). On the contrary, the exclusion of women on boards could have important negative effects on stakeholders, who may perceive the company to be pursuing discriminatory practices (Roberson and Park, 2007).

4.3. Psychological theories

Women and men have many different psychological traits. These can determine their behaviour and have important consequences on their decisions and actions. For that reason, there are a number of arguments from the sociology and psychology fields that must be taken into consideration to better understand the effects of gender diversity in boards of directors. Due to the recognised divergences in behavioural characteristics between males and females, the inclusion of women is likely to influence the way boards analyse information, deliberate, and make decisions (Gul et al., 2011).

First, female directors have been generally documented as having better interpersonal skills than their male counterparts, as showing greater trustworthiness, as carrying out a more participative communication style, and as enacting a more conciliatory leadership role (Eagly and Johnson, 1990; Daily and Dalton, 2003). Hence, these characteristics may have a significant impact on the decision-making process within a board as they are likely to create a good environment of communication and to encourage the board to consider different approaches and more varied opinions in a discussion (Heminway, 2007). In line with this, women may positively contribute to the way boards cope with complex decisions, thereby minimising informational biases in the formulation of corporate strategy (Francoeur et al., 2008).

On the other hand, in comparison with men, it is also widely recognised that women show less overconfidence and are more risk-adverse, thus being more conservative (Powell and Ansic, 1997; Man and Wong, 2013). This conservative mindset to a great extent implies that women have higher ethical standards and a greater sense of responsibility (Thorne et al., 2003; Pan and Sparks, 2012). Undoubtedly, these features suggest that female directors have a great propensity to fulfil their duties and perform their tasks effectively, among other matters, in order to minimise litigation risks and potential reputation loss (Srinidhi et al., 2011).

To sum up, these theories underline that all the psychological differences between men and women are relevant in order to understand the effects of female directors in the boardroom. This is why it is important to integrate this approach into the theoretical frameworks about board gender diversity since behavioural differences will significantly sharpen boards' decisions.

4.4. Resource dependence theory

According to resource dependence theory, the firm can be seen as a set of tangible and intangible resources and capabilities (Chambers et al., 2013). In this scenario, the board of directors can be considered as a key mechanism to guarantee the success of a firm, which must provide the CEO, the top executives, and the organisation as a whole with relevant resources (Pfeffer and Salancik, 1978). More specifically, the board of directors should provide valuable resources for the reduction of environmental uncertainty and the fulfilment of several tasks, including advising and counselling in the formulation of corporate strategy (Hillman and Dalziel, 2003). In other words, board members have an expectation and must be selected by means of criteria based on their background, contacts, and skills.

The literature on gender diversity has also considered the arguments extracted from resource dependence to explain the reasons behind the effects of women in the boardroom. For example, women are likely to provide the board with a wide set of resources, such as a greater range of expertise and competencies, and different leadership experiences (Quintana-García and Benavides-Velasco, 2016). These resources are particularly likely to promote greater creativity and hence more capacity to generate new ideas, and higher decision quality (Harrison and Klein, 2007).

On the other hand, gender diversity may also be important to expand the number of valuable links and improve networking, since women are essential to provide access to unique resources unreachable by their male counterparts (Siciliano, 1996). This argument is directly related with resource dependence theory since it states that gender-diverse boards can have valuable connections between the company and its environment.

In addition, one of the most important resources provided by women on boards is their cognitive style that empathises with organisational values and helps to create value (Krishnan and Park, 2005).

On the whole, this theory supports the need for gender diversity in boards, since female directors are providers of unique resources and firms may lose competitive advantages if they ignore female talent (Campbell and Mínguez-Vera, 2008).

4.5. Institutional theory

This theory considers that organisations are influenced by normative pressures, including those that are social and governmental (Zucker, 1987). In this sense, the configuration of corporate governance structures should be affected by external pressures. Under this rationale, the composition of the board of directors is expected to be influenced by social or political expectations. Given the ongoing discussions focused on gender equality, this theory is particularly interesting to provide a suitable framework for the analysis of the representation of women in the boardroom (Carrasco et al., 2015). Beyond female participation on boards of directors, institutional theory has become widespread in the analysis of the presence of women at other levels in the firm, in the political sphere, and in the labour market in general (Cabrera et al., 2016).

The classic argument rests on the idea that the presence of women in top management levels brings important benefits for firms because they gain symbolic legitimacy (Blum et al., 1994). In this sense, it is clear that women in top positions help to increase social legitimacy because this is a sign of the level of a firm's commitment to the progress of women at all levels (Daily and Dalton, 2003). And there is no need to say that gaining legitimacy helps in achieving important corporate outcomes.

4.6. Stewardship theory

Conversely to agency theory, stewardship theory assumes that the interests of boards of directors and managers are aligned, and both sets of actors take the best interests of the shareholders into consideration in their actions (Davis et al., 1997). In this context, managers are intrinsically motivated by intangible incentives, such as the possibility of attaining personal growth, and therefore managers and owners have common goals. As a result, the focus of the board of directors should be aiding the development of corporate strategies rather than monitoring managers' decisions.

The use of this theory in gender research is more limited. The few studies that employ stewardship theory to explain the role of female directors tend to assume that women behave as the stewards of the interests of firms. In this sense, female directors should reduce the problems and disagreements between the board members in order to make the board more proactive in improving the collaboration with managers (Nielsen and Huse, 2010). This framework rests on the premise that female directors are hard-working, responsible, and highly competent, these attributes being relevant in making the board work as a united team and improving the decision-making process to achieve a firm's main objectives. Basically, these are the arguments derived from stewardship theory to justify the presence of female members enhancing the ability of boards to implement company strategies.

4.7. Signalling theory

Despite being frequently used in the management and entrepreneur literature, this theory has been scarcely used in gender studies. The main assumption of signalling theory is the notion that firms disclose observable signals that are meaningful to the markets (Bear et al., 2010).

Regarding this, a firm can decide to select a more diverse board to communicate adherence to social values and enhance its reputation (Miller and Triana, 2009). This argument is closer to the reasons derived from institutional theory. In this case, companies do not increase the number of women to satisfy external pressures, but to voluntarily signal their socially responsible behaviour. In a few words, the company might be interesting in demonstrating its concern for the advancement of women and minorities. Indeed, companies with greater percentages of female directors are more likely to display pictures of them in their annual reports (Bernardi et al., 2009). Consistent with this approach, a firm may also benefit from a greater gender board diversity because it may make firms have more favourable investor perceptions and a better corporate reputation.

4.8. Tokenism perspective

Although female board representation might bring certain benefits, there are also theoretical arguments that can explain the existence of negative effects derived from an increased female participation in the boardroom. In this regard, when the presence of women on boards is a minority and can be explained due to external pressures (legal requirements, systems of quotas, corporate governance codes, or even social expectations), these female directors might be considered as tokens (Zelechowski and Bilimoria, 2004). The presence of women on the board as tokens, who are appointed based on external social or legal pressures rather than merits or qualifications, can lead to important internal conflicts and the influence of female directors might become negligible since they play out a mere institutional role (Campbell and Mínguez-Vera, 2008).

The theory of tokenism suggests that female directors can face important minority problems that could significantly harm their ability to make decisions and contribute to the boardroom (Elstad and Ladegard, 2012). First, women can perceive higher pressure and scrutiny than male board members, who are the dominant part. In addition, female minorities can also be excluded from informal networks and be forced into conventional categories defined by male directors. This will create huge barriers in women's ability to influence board decisions. For instance, gender minority directors tend to speak up less than other directors in board meetings and their contributions are less likely to be easily expressed or heard on the board (Westphal and Milton, 2000). Under this scenario, women may be perceived as a minority on boards, with less competence and lower status, and as a result, their opinions are also more likely to be less seriously considered by the board (Lord and Saenz, 1985).

Moreover, gender diversity can be negatively valued by the financial markets, especially if female directors are perceived as a minority appointed by external pressures (Hillman, 2015). From the idea that the investment profession has been historically controlled by men, capital markets can become biased against companies with greater gender board diversity if investors think that this gender minority, mainly seen as tokens, will hurt the firm's future performance.

4.9. Group phenomena perspective

Beyond the negative consequences on firm outcomes that board gender diversity may generate because the selection of women employing criteria in order to fulfil external demands or because of their consideration as tokens, studies from different social sciences fields have employed a group phenomena perspective in order to explain that female directors might also have a negative impact on board functioning.

On the one hand, social psychology research has extensively advocated that fault lines or hypothetical lines divide a group into smaller subgroups that are relatively homogeneous based on demographic characteristics, such as gender, age, or race (Lau and Murnighan, 1998).

Although there is no convincing theory to explain why subgroups in top management should form along sex categories rather than other director features, the literature supports that gender differences contribute to the creation of significant subgroups within the board of directors and this is expected to have harmful effects on the decision-making processes (Zhu et al., 2014). The existence of diverse groups within the board affects the director's ability to process and analyse the information about the firm and its environment. Indeed, empirical evidence has suggested that when female directors fail to reach a significant proportion in the board and become a critical mass of women (i.e., at least three), they have difficulties asking challenging questions and they may also find handicaps to work together and demonstrate collaboration in decision-making processes (Konrad et al., 2008).

On the other hand, diversity in the boardroom increases heterogeneity. This can lead to expressing divergent and contradictory opinions, and in turn may cause tension and internal conflicts (Stasser and Birchmeier, 2003). In this sense, directors are less capable of reaching a consensus concerning important issues, making the decision-making process and the settling of plans and strategies by managers more difficult (Williams and O'Reilly, 1998). Consistent with this approach, a number of studies have highlighted that gender diversity leads to a reduction in team cohesion, an increase in the volume of information discussed in board meetings and longer decision processes, consequently hindering firm performance and the team's ability to perform well and make better decisions (Horwitz and Horwitz, 2007; Mensi, 2014).

To sum up, under this group phenomena perspective, female board representation could worsen the board's cohesion and commitment. Thus, regardless of the particular skills or competences of women directors, gender board diversity can also be detrimental for a firm.

5 Measures for gender board diversity

As commented on throughout the previous chapters, in recent years, gender diversity on boards has turned out to be a crucial component of corporate governance structures (Terjesen et al., 2009) and, as a consequence, studies on gender board composition have proliferated. The search for accurate and comparable measures of gender board diversity is crucial to guarantee the reliability of the results found. In fact, important methodological requirements in this kind of research relate to the use of valid measures for female board representation. According to the existing literature, several measures for gender board composition have been commonly accepted in order to capture the degree of female participation on boards of directors.

In this section, we make a quick review of the main gender board diversity measures. This will be helpful for academics and researchers to both understand this topic and develop further investigation. First, intuitive measures, of a more basic nature, are commented on. Later, particular gender indices are described together with other specific measures. Finally, a set of proxies or indirect measures for gender board diversity is provided.

Traditionally, the measure most employed has been the percentage of female board members, or even the number of women in the board of directors. These are simple measures for gender board composition which have been extensively adopted by many authors (e.g., Adams and Ferreira, 2009; Campbell and Mínguez-Vera, 2008; Manita et al., 2018; Bravo and Reguera-Alvarado, 2019). Specifically, the proportion or percentage of female board members is calculated just as the ratio between the number of women directors and the total number of board members.

Another measure to capture gender diversity is defined by the critical mass theory (Kanter, 1977). This suggests that the nature of group interactions depends upon size. So, when a subgroup achieves a concrete size that is considered a determinant threshold or critical mass, the influence of this subgroup increases significantly. According to this theory, the literature has often employed a dummy variable to capture if there is a significant influence of a subgroup which is associated with female directors on the board. There are some authors who consider at least three women as the critical mass (Konrad et al., 2008; Kramer et al., 2006) because they reckon that three or more women in a board are able to ask challenging questions and demonstrate collaboration to work together in decision-making (Konrad et al., 2008; Kramer et al., 2006). In addition, in order to take the critical mass of women in boards in an empirical model into account, a set of dummy variables has also been employed by other authors (e.g., Kanter, 1977; Torchia et al., 2011; Liu et al., 2014; Manita et al., 2018). Thus, they define a first dummy variable that takes the value of 1 if there is one woman director and 0 otherwise, another dummy variable which takes the value of 1 if there are two female directors and 0 otherwise, and finally, a third dummy variable equals 1 if there are at least three female directors and 0 otherwise.

On the other hand, the use of gender diversity indices has become widespread in the gender literature (Campbell and Mínguez-Vera, 2008; Wilson, 2014; Abad et al., 2017; Ali and Konrad, 2017; Reguera-Alvarado et al., 2018). In general, a diversity index is a quantitative measure that reflects how many different types there are in a community, and simultaneously considers how equal the distribution is among those types. As a result, diversity indices may be employed in many different fields for assessing the diversity of any population in which each individual belongs to a unique group. Diversity indices are particularly used across fields such as sociology (Lieberson, 1969), ecology (Solow and Polasky, 1994), demography (Pelled, 1996), and economics (Dissart, 2003).

In relation to gender board diversity, the most common gender indices employed to capture female representation on boards are the Blau index (Blau, 1977) and the Shannon index. The Blau index, also known as Hirschman's and Herfindahl's index (Herfindahl, 1950; Hirschman, 1964), was originally developed by Simpson (1949) to quantify diversity between species and has become the most commonly used measure for gender diversity (Harrison and Klein, 2007). On the other hand, the Shannon index was developed by Claude Shannon and Warren Weaver in the late 1940s to quantify entropy (uncertainty or information content) in strings of text. Both indexes are very similar, but the Shannon index is more sensitive to small differences in the board's gender composition (Baumgärtner, 2006).

The Blau index considers, as a measure for gender diversity, both the number of gender categories (these categories are women and men) and the evenness of the distribution of board members between them. It is possible to combine these two attributes of diversity – which apply to "variety" and "balance", respectively – into "dual concept" measures of diversity (Stirling, 1998). The Blau index is measured as $\sum_{i=}^{n} 1 - P_i^2$, where "Pi" is the percentage of board members in each category and "n" is the total number of board members. The values of the Blau index for gender diversity vary from 0 to a maximum of 0.5. The latter score is awarded when the board of directors has an equal number of men and women.

The Shannon index is calculated as $- \sum_{i=}^{n} P_i * \ln(P_i) \ln P_i s$, where "P_i" and "n" have the same meaning as in the previous expression. Here the minimum value of the index is also 0 and diversity is at a maximum when there is an equal presence of both genders, which results in a value of 0.69. This index is more sensitive to any variation because it is based on a logarithmic measure and it explains both the abundance and evenness of the species present. The Shannon index adopts three assumptions: (1) All individuals are randomly sampled; (2) The population is indefinitely large, or effectively infinite; and (3) All species in the community are represented. It is not an appropriate measure when it is used with many communities, that is, when they are very diverse, or when the sample is very incomplete because the results tend to contain significant errors and bias.

In order to understand how to calculate both indexes, a number of examples are provided below.

Example 1

We suppose the following data about the distribution of directors between genders:

Percentage women = 30%
Percentage men = 70%

In order to calculate the Blau index we employ this equation:

Blau index = 1 – (Percentage women^2 + Percentage men^2) = 1 – (0.30^2 + 0.70^2) = 0.42

Example 2

In the case of the percentage of women being equal to the percentage of directors (i.e., 50% of representation for each gender), this means there is the maximum level of equality and the Blau index takes its maximum value, which is 0.5. For example:

Percentage women = 50%
Percentage men = 50%

Blau index = 1 − (Percentage women^2 +
Percentage men^2) = 1− (0.50^2 + 0.50^2) = 0.50

Example 3

On the other hand, if one of the two genders is not represented on the board, the Blau index would take its minimum value, which is 0. For example:

Percentage women = 0%
Percentage men = 100%

Blau index = 1 − (Percentage women^2 +
Percentage men^2) = 1 − (1^2) = 0

Now, we consider the previous examples to calculate the Shannon index.

Example 4

Percentage women = 30%
Percentage men = 70%

In order to calculate the Shannon index we employ this equation:

Shannon index = −1 * (((Percentage women* ln
(Percentage women)) + ((Percentage
men* ln (Percentage men))) = −
1* (((0.30 * ln (0.30) + (0.70 * ln
(0.70))) = 0.61

Example 5

For instance, if the percentage of women is equal to the percentage of directors (i.e., 50% of representation for each gender), this means there is the maximum level of equality and the Shannon index takes its maximum value, which is 0.69. For example:

Percentage women = 50%
Percentage men = 50%

Shannon index = −1 * (((Percentage women* ln (Percentage women)) + ((Percentage men* ln (Percentage men))) = −1* (((0.50 * ln (0.50) + (0.50 * ln (0.50))) = 0.69

Example 6

Finally, if one of the two genders is not represented on the board the Shannon index would take its minimum value, which is 0. For example:

Percentage women = 0%
Percentage men = 100%

Shannon index = −1 * (((Percentage women* ln (Percentage women)) + ((Percentage men* ln (Percentage men))) = −1* (1 * ln (1)) = 0

On the other hand, in addition to the basic measures and the gender indices, a number of proxies or indirect measures for gender board diversity have also been used in the literature as a consequence of the potential endogeneity concerns regarding the analysis of gender board composition in different firm-level outcomes. Hence, the previous literature has indicated the existence of a possible problem of endogeneity[1] when analysing linkages between gender diversity and some variables, such as disclosure information (Abernathy et al., 2013; Dou et al., 2015), financial performance (Adams and Ferreira 2009; Campbell and Mínguez-Vera 2008; Reguera-Alvarado et al., 2017; Srinidhi et al., 2011), and portfolio credit risk (Srinidhi et al., 2011), among other variables. In order to address this problem, the majority of authors have used a two-stage least squares regression. As upheld by Larcker and Rusticus (2010), this method requires the inclusion of instrumental variables which must be exogenous, unrelated to the firm-level outcomes but significantly correlated with the endogenous variable, in this case gender board diversity. Despite the difficulties of finding a valid instrument in general and for gender diversity in particular, the prior research has defined a set of instrumental variables that are considered proxies for gender board composition, for example the following:

- The visibility of the firm, which may be measured by taking into consideration its inclusion in a main stock market, is likely to determine female board participation. In fact, some authors have considered that firms listed in stock indices are expected to have a higher visibility and, accordingly, these firms are more exposed to pressures from investors, media, activists, etc. (Garcia-Castro et al., 2010), which influences the number of women in the boardroom.
- The second proxy refers to the social networks of the male board members, understood as the additional board positions occupied by male directors. This is generally measured as the proportion of male directors of a firm who sit on other boards that have at least one female director (Adams and Ferreira, 2009). In theory, male directors who work with women on other boards are more likely to facilitate the promotion of female directors.
- Another proxy for gender board composition can be board members' compensation. In this sense, the previous literature tends to indicate that a moderate compensation for directors is normally aligned with the recommendations from codes of good governance and usually engages in socially responsible behaviours of firms (Adams and Ferreira, 2009; Garcia-Castro et al., 2010). Consequently, companies with a moderate compensation of their board members are more likely to follow the good governance practices and will usually include greater board gender diversity.
- The existence of a gender quota law can be used to measure the presence of women on the board of directors. As was previously argued, some countries (e.g., France, Germany, Canada, Denmark, and Austria) have introduced mandatory gender quotas to obligate companies to have a minimum number of female directors on the board. The implementation of these laws requires an increase in the representation of female directors. So, the target or percentage of women directors is expected to be higher in the years following the enactment of these laws. Therefore, a valid instrumental variable may be a dummy variable dividing with the value of 0 for a firm in

the years before the mandatory law and the value of 1 just after its enactment (Reguera-Alvarado et al., 2017).

- The proportion of female managers (Low et al., 2015) and the percentage of women in the industry (Liu et al., 2014) have been also proxies for female participation, assuming that both factors reflect a corporate culture more inclined to favouring advances in women's professional careers.

- Even the education of the CEO has been considered an indirect measure of female board representation (Smith et al., 2006), as it can determine his/her attitude towards women directors.

In summary, many measures for gender board diversity have been commonly accepted in the previous literature and are available for researchers. Their inclusion in empirical studies should be done carefully, because some mixed results may appear due to the use of different measures. Therefore, we highly recommend further research to carry out sensitivity analyses. These consider various gender diversity measures simultaneously in empirical research in order to confirm the robustness of results irrespective of the isolated use of only one measure.

In the same way that regulations tend to take into account just the presence of women in the boardroom rather than the specific powerful positions occupied by female directors, the vast majority of gender diversity measures only strictly focus on female board representation. Obviously, this may be a limitation in the understanding of how female directors can influence decision-making processes. At the same time, this can be considered as a great opportunity for academics to develop more comprehensive measures that aggregate both the presence of women in boards of directors and their actual power in the boardroom, considering for example the board titles they have, whether they participate in specific board subcommittees, or whether they are the chairwoman of the board or its committees, or the CEO.

Note

1 Endogeneity problems occur due to omitted variables and selection biases, mis-specified or erroneous variables, measurement errors, and joint simultaneity (Verbeek, 2008).

6 The effect of board gender composition

Empirical evidence

Along with including gender issues in the political and social agenda, empirical research on gender diversity has become widespread. A good proof of this is the number of studies that have proliferated worldwide. For example, a quick search in Google Scholar for the terms *gender diversity* generates about 3 million hits. In particular, a significant proportion of these papers are related to corporate governance and deal with the role of women in the governance structures of firms. Searching for the terms *board gender diversity* yields almost 2 million studies. It is particularly interesting to highlight the evolution of this research, since the number of studies has been especially high in the current century, specifically in the last decade. These figures illustrate that gender board composition has gained a great deal of attention among academics in recent years. But far from becoming stagnant, public and private organisations claim the need for further research on gender diversity in general, including an in-depth analysis of the role of female board members. In general, research on female directors remains important because it develops an accurate picture of how the actual situation is and contributes to better refined arguments about the effects of board gender diversity. This academic trend can also be observed by looking at the most valued indicators of research publications,[1] the Journal Citation Report (JCR) and Scimago Journal Rank (SJR). Indeed, the number of journals included in gender categories from both indicators continues to increase and has become significant. For instance, in 2018, the JCR category related to women studies contains 44 journals, and the SJR category referring to gender studies is made up of 131 journals.

Logically, given the multidisciplinary nature of gender issues, the previous studies belong to many different research fields. A very recent review of the studies about gender diversity (Kirsch, 2018) reveals that the majority of the articles appear in journals in the fields of corporate governance, business, management, ethics, and finance and accounting, although some articles have been also published in other areas such as law, economics, human resource management, strategy, and organisational behaviour. With reference to the authorship of these studies, it is interesting to stress that this topic has attracted similar attention from women and men, as the number of articles about gender diversity carried out by female and male researchers seems to be similar. It is also relevant to indicate that most of these studies are carried out on a single country, predominantly Anglo-Saxon regions and those countries where gender diversity on boards was first incorporated into the political agenda and came into legislation, such as Norway or Spain. This can be seen as a limitation that may harm the generalisability of the evidence found due to the divergences between the institutional contexts and cultural issues across countries.

The first studies about gender diversity date from many decades ago, and the most important academic journals started publishing articles regarding gender diversity and corporate governance in the past century, around the 1970s. The progress of this branch of research can be broken down into different stages (Joshi et al., 2015; Kirsch, 2018). In the first years, researchers began to focus on the plight of and barriers for women in the business sphere, with the purpose of describing the existing situation and underlining the discriminatory situation of women in the economic world. For example, in the 1980s and early 1990s researchers started to report detailed statistics about the presence of women on boards and to scrutinise the main features of industries, companies, and boards that tended to have female directors, in order to search for the existence of patterns that could explain the participation of women in top business positions. During this time, many studies investigated the nature of the recruitment and selection of female directors. Later, in the 1990s, researchers began to deal with the effects of women on boards. The goal of this stream of research was to analyse whether the presence of women might change processes or dynamics. More recent studies place a strong emphasis on the impact of women in top business positions on many different firm outcomes. Consistent with this idea, in the late 1990s and the current century, attention turned to the effects of board gender diversity on firm financial performance and corporate strategy, among other firm outcomes.

This branch of studies focusing on the effects of board gender composition aims to address the wide discussion concerning the real economic impact of women in top business positions. The major debate in this area is whether the presence of women in governance structures may really have a positive influence on the functioning of the boards, on decision-making processes, the implementation of specific actions and, ultimately, corporate performance (Adams and Ferreira, 2009). As was explained in the section about the theoretical approach, a number of theories support that greater gender diversity, due to many different reasons, may lead to better corporate governance practices, improved stakeholder relations, and more effective corporate strategies. This, in turn, will result in enhanced financial performance. Taking these theoretical arguments into consideration, the impact of female directors on a number of firm outcomes has been largely analysed in the literature.

The main objective of this section is to summarise the empirical evidence found concerning the effects of female directors within the board or its committees. This section aims to provide an overview of this topic, which is likely to be a useful tool for academics and society to ascertain the situation concerning the existing findings, and guide future research to reach more conclusive evidence. To that end, this chapter contains several headings that review the main conclusions extracted from previous studies on the effects of board gender composition.

First, the most primary studies examine the potential relationship between gender board diversity and a basic firm-level outcome, such as financial performance. The evidence is mixed and different reasons, which will be described further, can be provided to explain the inconclusive findings. In particular, one of the criticisms of these kinds of studies is the difficulty of justifying the causal path to explain the direct effects of gender diversity on boards on financial performance. Accordingly, scholars are increasingly investigating how the gender of directors affects interactions on the board as a group and, as a consequence, board decisions concerning specific firm strategies, and, ultimately, firm financial performance. On this subject, researchers have started to include more nuanced variables and more proximal outcomes than firm performance, focusing on particular corporate decisions. Therefore, the analysis of the impact of female directors on corporate social responsibility (CSR) and specific firm strategies has become widespread. Besides, recent research trends emphasise the need to consider the context in which female directors work and, as a result, employ a contextual or contingency analysis to really comprehend the way women make decisions and influence the board's behaviour. Furthermore, we also remark that mere gender per se may be insufficient to understand the effects of female directors in decision-making processes and firm outcomes. In this sense, researchers are currently claiming for the need to carry out an in-depth analysis of the characteristics of female directors, since the education, experience, age, tenure, or positions occupied by women, among other things, are likely to determine their behaviour and their influence.

Obviously, all these issues need to be taken into account in order to open up the black box regarding the actual impact of board gender composition. In the following sections, we summarise the empirical evidence found concerning each of these aspects, and present several headings to do with the following topics: (1) the effects of board gender composition on firm performance; (2) the effects of board gender composition on CSR; (3) the effects of board gender composition on specific firm strategies; (4) the importance of using a contextual approach to know how some external and internal factors can moderate the influence of female directors; (5) the effect of particular characteristics of women directors on their decision-making process.

6.1. Board gender diversity and firm financial performance

Many papers have examined the relationship between female participation in boards of directors and the financial performance of firms. This is because of the impulse provided by the theoretical foundations (commented on in the previous chapters) that establish a link between gender diversity and business outcomes, given that financial performance is a basic firm-level outcome. Nevertheless, the results are far from definitive, and empirical evidence is inconclusive. Many studies have documented the existence of a positive association between board gender diversity and firm financial performance (Carter et al., 2003; Campbell and Mínguez-Vera, 2008; Amore et al., 2014; Low et al., 2015; Reguera-Alvarado et al., 2017). At the same time, other studies support the existence of a neutral association between gender diversity and firm performance (Kochan et al., 2003; Rose, 2007; Isidro and Sobral, 2015) and even a negative relationship (Du Rietz and Henrekson, 2000; Bøhren and Strøm, 2010; Ujunwa, 2012; Joecks et al., 2013).

Although there is not a complete consensus on the reasons that may explain these contradictory findings, this evidence calls into question the theoretical approaches concerning the benefits of female members in corporate governance structures. Given the relevance of this issue, researchers have also addressed why the findings are inconclusive, and recent trends support that the mixed results found might be to a great extent explained by methodological aspects (Cabrera-Fernández et al., 2016). As most of these studies employ econometric analysis to examine the effect of board gender composition on firm performance, changes in the research method might bias the results obtained. Therefore, the question is: what are the methodological matters that should be taken into consideration?

In this sense, it is easy to understand that the use of different time periods or samples from different countries is likely to affect the results obtained by researchers. The regulation of corporate governance mechanisms, the culture, the functioning of the financial markets, and the economic environment will be different in every country. In other words, the empirical evidence is highly dependent on the economic context. In addition, there are also significant divergences in the samples because of the types of firms included. For instance, the role of female directors varies whether the analysis focuses on one specific industry or on firms with a dissimilar size.

Other methodological issues that can explain the existence of mixed results are related to the size of the samples used and the design of the variables. As commented in the previous sections, board gender diversity can be measured in different ways, as well as financial performance. On the one hand, the use of variables based on the proportion of women on boards could be insufficient to capture the effect of female directors, especially when the number of women in the boardroom is low and a critical mass of female board members is not reached. The appointment of only one or two female directors is unlikely to change board dynamics because women are seen as a minority, and this will prevent the potential benefits of gender diversity, thus introducing an important bias in the empirical analysis. Therefore, in order to increase the comparability and the reliability of the results obtained, it would be advisable to carry out sensibility analysis and use suitable samples with a critical mass of women to capture the actual effect of female directors. On the other hand, moving on to the main variables used to measure financial performance, researchers have alternatively employed different measures, hence affecting the comparability across studies, such as the following ratios: return on equity ratio, return on investment, return on assets, return on capital invested, price to book ratio, or Tobin's Q, among others.

In addition to these methodological aspects, endogeneity has become a significant concern in corporate governance studies and specific analysis to deal with endogeneity problems needs to be incorporated to avoid bias in the results obtained. Specifically, in the analysis of the effect of women in the boardroom, there are two reasons why endogeneity issues may arise: the existence of omitted unobservable variables and reverse causality. Not paying attention to these problems can significantly confound the interpretation of the evidence noted in the empirical studies.

On the one hand, omitted variables that affect both the selection of female directors and firm outcomes could lead to spurious correlations. Regarding this, it would be plausible for the determinants of firm performance and other firm outcomes to be the same as the drivers of better corporate governance structures and therefore the level of board gender composition. There are many cases of exogenous variables in experimental designs that correlate with both the dependent and independent variables and a classic example for explaining this issue could be the old association between ice cream sales and murder rates in the United States (www.psychologyinaction.org/psychology-in-action-1/2011/10/30/what-is-a-confounding-variable). It is clear that both variables are unrelated, nevertheless, an additional variable, heat, can be responsible for them. Therefore, there might be an external variable that impacts on both women board selection and financial performance.

On the other hand, reverse causality means that the selection of board members with certain attributes is probably not random and that firm outcomes may influence board structures (Armstrong et al., 2014; Carcello et al., 2006). This would imply that individuals self-select boards where they serve based on certain characteristics. For example, women can select boards from firms with better firm performance and other financial or social outcomes so that they can build their reputations and avoid undertaking an additional workload. In conclusion, researchers must control for the direction of causality to make sure that female board representation leads to enhanced financial performance rather than the other way around.

The recent literature highlights that the complexity of controlling these endogeneity problems (reverse causation and the existence of other omitted variables that may be affecting both board diversity and firm outcomes) can be crucial in the results obtained in empirical research. Indeed, recent studies emphasise the need to cope with this problem and researchers provide valuable insights and offer a range of potential solutions to alleviate endogeneity concerns in the analysis of the effects of directors. The literature generally considers alternative methodological analyses to minimise endogeneity, such as the use of instrumental variables, Generalised Method of Moments (GMM), 2 Stage Least Squares (SLS).

In the light of these concerns, the search for comparable and accurate methodologies seems to be necessary for empirical studies to contribute to the active political, economical, and societal debates, which will obviously benefit from more conclusive evidence. Under this scenario of mixed findings, despite the theoretical perspectives supporting the financial benefits of gender diversity in boards and the number of studies documenting a positive link between the presence of female directors and firm financial performance, the actual facts show that firms are to a certain extent reluctant to trust this relationship. On balance, the previous literature tends to advocate that board gender diversity adds more to a firm than it takes away (Grosvold et al., 2016), and gender diversity has undoubtedly become a priority for regulators and academics. However, researchers must provide more convincing arguments to make this a reality in the business world.

The descriptive map described in the previous sections reveals that the proportion of female board members has increased recently, but slighter than might have been expected some years ago. If companies really perceived important benefits driven by an increase in board gender diversity, the number of female directors would have rapidly increased in the last years, even without the need of imposing quotas or pushing firms by soft laws or recommendations. This situation leads us to think about what is behind a firm's board selection process and formulate the same questions as researchers did many years ago: is gender diversity in boards determined by an economic rationale or by moral justice reasons?

6.2. Board gender diversity and corporate social responsibility

The Green Paper of the European Commission (European Commission, 2001) defines CSR as "the voluntary integration of social and environmental concerns in their business operations and in their interaction with their stakeholders and to fully comply with applicable legal obligations, but also to go beyond and invest more in environmental human capital". CSR has become an extremely important issue for firms, policy-makers, and professional bodies, and has even been brought into the political agenda. Accordingly, the growth in the academic interest for CSR issues is irrefutable. In particular, in this century researchers have dramatically increased the number of studies dealing with CSR topics, paying special attention to the fulfilment of the relevant global voluntary regulations, codes, guidelines, and initiatives, such as the Global Reporting Initiative (GRI) or the UN Global Compact (Tripahi and Bains, 2013). The evolution of this line of research is clear: while initially some authors and companies tended to generally think that CSR actions were irrelevant and expensive corporate strategy, CSR initiatives have recently been considered a key business strategy for an organisation's success. In fact, addressing social issues is increasingly perceived as an effective way to gain competitive advantage for firms.

As CSR is by nature a cross-curricular subject, studies on this topic have been published in many different research areas. Nevertheless, we note the proliferation of papers examining potential associations between corporate governance aspects (and specifically board gender diversity) and CSR issues. This can be possibly explained by social issues, including those referring to environmental changes, social inclusion, governance, and gender parity, being among the most pressing global challenges that must be faced by the various economic actors in the current century (World Economic Forum, 2016). In this regard, a significant number of studies have pointed to the board of directors as responsible for improving different CSR outcomes. One of the most recommended solution is to increase the proportion of female directors, under the assumption that the experience and values of women are likely to positively impact CSR. In this sense, researchers seem to reach a consensus on the greater orientation of women towards environmental and social issues (Agarwal, 2010; Kaijser and Kronsell, 2014) and, as a result, modern studies have been based on these ideas to investigate the potential effect of gender board composition on CSR practices (Horbach and Jacob, 2018). However, the empirical evidence is mixed and still far from conclusive. Next, we provide a brief description about the research that has been done to examine this topic.

First, a recent review carried out by Byron and Post (2016), who performed a meta-analysis of international studies, indicates that empirical studies confirm that the effect of women directors on corporate social performance is generally positive. Certainly, the evidence about the impact of female directors on social aspects is less equivocal than the proof regarding the connection between women directors and financial performance effects. All the same, these authors suggest that a deeper investigation should be done to comprehend the reasons behind the previous relationship to better understand the role of women in the boardroom in improving CSR performance and strategies. For instance, by addressing the questions about which CSR actions are likely to be intensified by female board members or which women features may help to improve CSR practices. In order to do so, qualitative research can be a very useful tool to find an answer to explain what really occurs. Focusing on CSR practices, researchers usually consider variables related to CSR performance, centred on the actions taken by firms and the perception from stakeholders, and related to CSR reporting, an important CSR outcome to legitimise the behaviour of firms.

On the other hand, studies that have examined the effect of women directors on CSR performance generally employ CSR ratings (Bear et al., 2010; Harjoto et al., 2015; Glass et al., 2016; Zhang et al., 2018). These ratings focus on similar CSR dimensions and have been widely used in the academic literature. Among these ratings, many authors have used KLD scores or Asset4 scores. For example, KLD ratings include the assessment of the performance of firms in different areas such as community, corporate governance, diversity, employee relations, product, and environmental issues. Meanwhile, CSR performance indicators obtained from Thomson Reuters ASSET4 provide assessment about a company's environmental, social, and governance performance. These kinds of scores are very useful tools for research since the analysts transform qualitative data concerning the CSR behaviour of firms into quantitative variables (Ioannou and Serafeim, 2015).

Beyond CSR performance, numerous studies have focused on the impact of female directors on CSR reporting strategy. In particular, recent research has suggested that the presence of women on boards is linked to improvements in the extent of the overall CSR information or the disclosure of specific CSR information (Arayssi et al., 2016; Rao and Tilt, 2016; Helfaya and Moussa, 2017). On this subject, different measures for CSR information have also been employed. For instance, some authors have used scores provided by specific organisations such as Bloomberg or the Carbon Disclosure Project (Ben Barka and Dardour, 2015; Bravo and Reguera-Alvarado, 2019), and others have carried out a content analysis of CSR reports (Rao et al., 2012; Giles and Murphy, 2016). In addition, several studies have also examined the influence of women directors on the fulfilment of international guidelines about reporting practices (i.e., the Global Reporting Initiative) or the assurance of CSR information (Amran et al., 2014; Al-Shaer and Zaman, 2018).

6.3. Board gender diversity and other business strategies

This section summarises the evidence reported in the previous research about the effects of board gender composition on concrete business strategies. This has also attracted a great deal of academic attention. As has been commented on in most of the previous sections, this line of literature relies on the commonly accepted assumption that the presence of women affects decision-making processes within a group and so female directors are expected to have an impact on particular management decisions. Logically, understanding the potential effect of board gender diversity on certain firm strategies remains a relevant question for companies and regulators alike. Regarding this, the previous literature has investigated whether female representation in boards of directors can exert an influence on specific corporate key decisions, such as those related to innovation, mergers and acquisitions, and financial disclosure practices, among others.

Decisions concerning innovation practices and research and development (R&D) investments, crucial to enhance competitive advantages of firms and critical for their long-term success, demand certain features from board members. Several studies find a positive effect of female directors on innovation because women help to broaden the skills in the boardroom and provide different experiences and perspectives, thus favouring the generation of new and innovative ideas (Van der Vegt and Janssen, 2003; Díaz-García et al., 2013; Quintana-García and Benavides-Velasco, 2016). Moreover, the particular characteristics of women, such as high sensitivity and closeness to stakeholders, can help to identify new needs and trends in the markets, thereby promoting R&D investments and the development of new products (Ritter-Hayashi et al., 2016). In the same way as we remarked in the previous sections, the previous evidence fails to be fully conclusive and the results to a certain extent depend on the measures of innovation and gender diversity employed by researchers, and on the existence of a critical mass of women directors with enough power to change board dynamics (Miller and Triana, 2009; Torchia et al., 2011; Galia and Zenou, 2012).

Other studies have also examined the effect of gender diversity on merger and acquisition strategies. These are also significant decisions in firms and require specific characteristics of board members. In this sense, some authors have found that boards with a higher female representation are, probably because of their risk aversion, more reluctant to make acquisitions (Levi et al., 2014; Chen et al., 2016).

Another relevant firm strategy that has been largely analysed concerns financial reporting practices. These become crucial in reducing information asymmetries, enhancing transparency and therefore improving the functioning of capital markets. Researchers generally document that female board members are more independent and perform better monitoring and, as a consequence, board gender composition may lead to better financial disclosures (Pucheta-Martínez et al., 2016; Abad et al., 2017).

The presence of women on boards has been also considered as a determinant of dividends policy. Although empirical evidence is more limited than in the previous cases, some studies show that gender diversity in the boardroom contributes to enhancing dividends payouts, suggesting that female directors use dividends payments as a governance device (Al-Rahahleh, 2017; Chen et al., 2017).

In addition, employment policies might be influenced by board gender composition. For instance, female directors are more prone to set up compensation mechanisms closely linked to firm performance (Lucas-Pérez et al., 2015) and to establish human resources policies closer to a social sensitiveness (Cook and Glass, 2016). What is more, some authors also demonstrate that gender diversity in boards reduces discrimination practices at the lower managerial levels (Skaggs et al.,

2012), and also mitigates the gender gap in executive compensation (Elkinawy and Stater, 2011).

Logically, there are many other corporate decisions that might be affected by the board gender composition, and the list could be endless. In this regard, and despite the limited number of studies on other firm strategies, the effect of board gender diversity has been analysed in the previous literature for concrete decisions regarding diverse topics such as a firm's degree of internationalisation (Rivas, 2012), customer orientation strategies (Hillman, 2015), and tax policy (Lanis et al., 2017), among others.

Therefore, as has been shown, this is an open field, which presents many future research avenues, since the presence of women on boards is expected to play an important role in the decisions made in relation to many relevant business strategies. The increase in the number of studies about the effect of gender diversity on specific strategies can perhaps serve as a significant theoretical support to unravel the impact of female board members and to understand the indirect effect of women in top business positions on firm financial performance.

6.4. A contextual approach: potential moderators of the influence of female directors

The recent literature seems to agree that it is unlikely that board members will uniformly affect decision-making processes and firm outcomes across all contexts. In particular, the extent to which female board representation can influence decision-making within the board and therefore corporate strategies and firm performance is likely to depend on the context in which they work (Byron and Post, 2016). In other words, female directors may prove to act differently depending on their environment. For that reason, research increasingly underlines the need to use a contextual or contingency approach as a valuable perspective to expand the understanding of board gender composition and to resolve prior inconclusive evidence (Ely et al., 2004; Bravo and Reguera-Alvarado, 2019). This view proves to be particularly valuable since decisions made within boards are significantly affected by the key contingency factors. These contextual factors comprise a broad range of aspects, including issues which are both internal and external to the firm. Although the literature regarding the moderating factors of gender diversity effects remains scarce, a few papers have examined whether the environment of female directors determines the way women act within the board. The premises underlying these studies tend to assume that companies may benefit more from gender diversity depending on firm-level characteristics or even intra-board features. Therefore, contextual factors must play a key role in explaining the effectiveness of gender diversity composition.

On the one hand, firm-level characteristics are likely to determine the role of board members and the way directors perform their tasks (Reguera-Alvarado and Bravo, 2018). In this sense, certain decisions regarding specific corporate strategies are significantly determined by a firm's inherent characteristics. So, it can be expected that the size of a firm, its leverage, growth options, sector, or its life stage can determine the objectives and decisions within the board of directors. Specifically, the literature on gender diversity has pointed out, for instance, that the industry in which a company operates (Li et al., 2017), its overall business strategy (Richard, 2000), and the firm size (Zona et al., 2013) are moderating factors of the influence of female board members on corporate decisions.

On the other hand, boards generally work as a group, and hence it is expected that global board characteristics will affect the way directors make decisions (Miller and Triana, 2009). Recent evidence shows that board features, such as their activity or frequency of meetings (Bravo and Reguera-Alvarado, 2019), are also likely to moderate the impact that women on boards may have on corporate decisions.

There is no doubt that future research should continue exploring the effect of female directors by using contextual analysis in order to advance the understanding of boards of directors. Furthermore, taking into account the lack of conclusive advancement in the research on boards, this contextual perspective may be useful to uncover specific effects of female directors, since gender diversity effects may be enhanced or restricted depending on the context in which the company operates. In addition, the role of female directors could also be moderated by other factors, such as CEO features and the very characteristics of women. As a result, this area presents promising research opportunities to improve our knowledge about the role of female board members.

6.5. The effect of women directors' particular characteristics

The majority of the previous studies consider the degree of gender representation in the board to examine the influence of female directors, assuming that gender per se exerts an effect on certain firm outcomes. However, a more in-depth analysis may be required in order to comprehend the true influence of women on boards. On this subject, the impact of female directors may, without considering their personal attributes, also lead to inconclusive results in the literature. The previous studies usually fail to carry out a detailed analysis of how the specific characteristics of female board members affect their contributions to the boardroom. Yet, it seems logical to think that personal features (i.e., background, maturity, expertise) are likely to influence the way women make decisions (Zelechowski and Bilimoria, 2004; Gull et al., 2018).

A few recent studies have begun questioning which individual characteristics might drive female directors to make more effective decisions. For instance, some authors indicate that female directors' functional expertise can improve board functioning (Kim and Starks, 2016). Business expertise can also help female directors to increase their involvement in certain corporate policies, such as reporting practices (Gull et al., 2018). In particular, recent studies have documented that female directors' specific financial expertise is a crucial attribute for them in improving financial disclosure strategies (Bravo and Alcaide-Ruiz, 2019). In addition to their expertise, the power of female board members is also considered to be determinant of their influence. The power of women directors is unlikely to be the same when they have different board or subcommittee titles or when they are in committee memberships (Triana et al., 2013). As a matter of fact, when female directors have an audit committee membership, they seem to be more proactive in developing better disclosure practices through mitigating earnings management (Gull et al., 2018). In addition, tenure may also be an important characteristic to understand the influence of women in the boardroom. It is well documented that female directors tend to experience shorter tenures than their male counterparts and logically this is likely to affect their ability to make decisions and contribute to the board's functioning (Main et al., 2018).

To sum up, research on this issue is still largely unexplored and a number of personal characteristics might be examined to understand in which circumstances women exert an effect on specific corporate decisions. Researchers have encouraging opportunities to conduct further investigation into the impact of the characteristics commented on above, concerning women's expertise, power, and tenure. Additionally, other aspects that should affect the ability of female directors to make certain decisions may also be considered, including their age, education and social background, ownership ties to the firm, number of directorships, and compensation, among many other features (Kirsch, 2018).

Note

1 Both JCR (published by Clarivate Analytics) and SJR (based on the SCOPUS database) provide information about the best academic journals in the natural sciences and social sciences, according to their impact factors, which are calculated by considering their number of citations.

7 Concluding remarks

In recent years, gender diversity has been the focus of politicians, policy-makers, professionals, and academics. The idea of women having to be represented at all levels has been emphasised throughout the previous chapters, and this message is making a deep impression on most societies. This calls for more advances concerning women's progress.

Undoubtedly, gender equality in a broad sense is also generally associated with gender fairness in the workplace. Accordingly, the voices of an important part of the citizenship and governments support the need to enhance the participation of women in the workforce. The majority of the reports show that women devote much more time to domestic duties, hence affecting their opportunities to fully develop a professional career. At the same time, cultural biases also affect the business world and discrimination remains in companies, in some cases it might even be intentionally so. As a matter of fact, gender equality in the workplace is still far from being reached. A disparity between women and men is especially significant in top business positions, which are precisely the most visible places in companies. Specifically, this book has centred on the situation regarding women in boards of directors. This is a controversial issue that has aroused a great deal of interest and sharpened intense debates from many different perspectives. Indeed, both regulators and academics have made significant efforts in recent years to better comprehend the effects of an increase in female representation on boards.

Many opinions claim that gender diversity in the boardroom does not need to be supported by only reasonableness or rational arguments, which to a certain extent could be determined by cultural biases and patriarchy. This should be a priority just because of justice or moral reasons. The inclusion of women in the boardroom can be a sign of commitment to gender equality and it is necessary in order to mitigate gender slants and discrimination policies. At the same time, a high presence of women in leadership posts would imply a significant step forward given that it might facilitate and stimulate gender equality policies at most of the business levels. This is likely to positively impact on long-term social welfare.

But, in addition to the ethical view on this issue, there are many experts who advocate that board gender diversity is also good for firms and society because of economic reasons. This argument tends to rely on the fact that female directors are likely to affect board decisions, and this may have a positive impact on a number of firm-level outcomes and, at a global level, on capital markets or even national GDP. In fact, empirical findings generally suggest that board gender composition has positive economic effects and this, together with the moral arguments, reinforces the policies currently being discussed or implemented by international organisations to promote the progress of women in leadership positions.

Nevertheless, the current figures still show an alarming scenario: the number of female board members remains low, and female directors are more likely to suffer all kinds of discrimination. First, despite the regulatory reforms concerning gender board composition, which have considerably increased in recent years, women on boards tend to be significantly underrepresented in most countries. Second, although the statistics indicate that women have slightly broken through the glass ceiling and reached top positions in firms, female directors are still more exposed to being treated in a discriminatory manner. Regarding this, women directors are less likely to hold board titles and this hinders them gaining power. In addition, female board members are often under closer scrutiny and, consequently, they tend to be undervalued in comparison to male directors.

The situation described inevitably leads one to wonder about the reasons behind this gender inequality. The regulatory actions go in the same direction: board gender composition has become a priority in corporate governance reforms. Empirical evidence also encourages enhancing female board representation, not only due to moral reasons, but also because of economic arguments. A significant number of researchers have stated that gender diversity can improve the quality of boards and therefore help to improve financial performance, social performance, and particular decisions regarding relevant corporate strategies, among other advantages. However, this does not seem enough to really enhance the participation of women in leadership positions. Why? Probably the reason is simple, many firms are reluctant to trust the current empirical evidence. Therefore, many managers may doubt whether it is really true that only including a few women on the board may provide such a powerful transformation. If so, firms might add women to the board just as a response to regulatory or societal pressures.

In the light of these circumstances, it seems clear that there is still a long way to go and efforts must be intensified, bringing together strong measures from different perspectives. In this sense, researchers are in a good position to further explore the role of women in leadership positions in order to obtain more conclusive and convincing results. Moreover, governments have a great opportunity to take proactive steps and make gender equality a reality.

On the one hand, researchers and academics all over the world need to be aware that equivocal methodologies and inconsistent evidence have possibly left companies and professional bodies puzzled. Sometimes, empirical studies have been criticized, claiming that authors may feel the temptation to fabricate results about the advantages of selecting more women in the boardroom. In order to dispel all the potential doubts, methodological approaches must be clear, robust, and replicable. More in-depth investigation is also required to have a big picture of the matter and to address some unanswered questions. On this subject, as more research is done, more questions arise, thereby providing interesting research avenues, which can also be relevant for companies and regulators. Just as an example, efforts may be increased to continue detailed analyses about the personal characteristics of female directors that can be more relevant in improving board effectiveness. Furthermore, it is also important to investigate whether the effects of gender board composition depend on the fact of gender diversity being a voluntary option or a legal requirement, since legal quotas, for instance, may lead to the isolation of female directors. Another question that requires more research is the analysis of the factors that can moderate the role of female board members, and how the context determines the actual influence of women in boards. In addition, the timing of board gender diversity is also a relevant question, given that the firms which are pioneers in this issue can enjoy different advantages than the rest. Moreover, existing research mainly focuses on larger and listed companies, but what happens with small and medium enterprises (SMEs)? These companies represent a high percentage of most economies, they contribute significantly to GDPs and the generation of employment, but the evidence concerning the influence of women in these firms is very rare. We hardly know anything about this, and the results found in research so far might not be valid for these kinds of firms. To sum up, there are many unsolved questions that present great opportunities to really unriddle the role of women on boards and shed some light on the benefits and costs of enhanced board gender diversity. On the other hand, governments have important challenges to face. Regardless of the strictly economic rationale that justifies female representation in top business positions because they can lead to superior firm-level outcomes, women need to be provided with the same opportunities to sit on a board as men. In other words, although the female economic contribution is similar to the male performance, women should not be affected by any kind of discrimination and their participation in boards of directors should have the same options as men only for reasons of fairness. What image is transmitted when most powerful positions are occupied by men? How can a society really develop in terms of equality if half of its population lacks representation in leadership positions?

In light of this reality, governments have the power to take active and decisive steps to implement strong policies to improve work–life balance, to implement gender policies in many kinds of institutions and organisations and to make the access of women to leadership positions easier. Further, one of the most important actions to be taken has to do with education. This is clearly crucial to fight against stereotypes and discrimination practices, and to raise global awareness of the need to consider gender diversity as important. Managers must be convinced that if firms fail to integrate women into leadership posts, they can become outdated and they are missing out on great opportunities. It is key to continue working in this direction and gain ground to make all advances concerning gender equality in the workplace irreversible. Particularly, taking advantage of the current trends, this is an excellent moment to implement and consolidate the measures necessary to achieve gender equality at all levels and, specifically, to banish the problem of gender diversity in top business positions. In summary, progress is evident, but it is time to carry out a profound reflection about the changes that must be made to attain effective gender equality in corporate governance mechanisms. First, continuous efforts are necessary to guarantee that the current trends remain in the future and to enhance awareness of this issue at all levels. Besides, in order to achieve actual gender equality, the measures and actions taken must consider not only equal representation in governance structures, but equal participation in power.

Bibliography

Abad, D., Lucas-Pérez, M. E., Mínguez-Vera, A., & Yagüe, J. (2017). Does gender diversity on corporate boards reduce information asymmetry in equity markets? *Business Research Quarterly*, 20(3), 192–205.

Abernathy, J. L., Herrmann, D., Kang, T., & Krishnan, G. V. (2013). Audit committee financial expertise and properties of analyst earnings forecasts. *Advances in Accounting*, 29(1), 1–11.

Adams, R. B., de Haan, J., Terjesen, S., & van Ees, H. (2015). Board diversity: Moving the field forward. *Corporate Governance: An International Review*, 23(2), 77–82.

Adams, R. B., & Ferreira, D. (2009). Women in the boardroom and their impact on governance and performance. *Journal of Financial Economics*, 94(2), 291–309.

Adams, R. B., & Kirchmaier, T. (2015). Barriers to boardrooms. ECGI – Finance Working Paper No. 347/2013. Asian Finance Association (AsFA) 2013 Conference.

Adler, N. J., & Izraeli, D. N. (1994). *Competitive frontiers*. Cambridge, MA: Blackwell.

Agarwal, B. (2010). *Gender and green governance*. Oxford: Oxford University Press.

Aguilera, R. V., & Cuervo-Cazurra, A. (2009). Codes of good governance. *Corporate Governance: An International Review*, 17(3), 376–387.

Ali, M., & Konrad, A. M. (2017). Antecedents and consequences of diversity and equality management systems: The importance of gender diversity in the TMT and lower to middle management. *European Management Journal*, 35, 440–453.

Al-Rahahleh, A. S. (2017). Corporate governance quality, board gender diversity and corporate dividend policy: Evidence from Jordan. *Australasian Accounting, Business and Finance Journal*, 11(2), 86–104.

Al-Shaer, H., & Zaman, M. (2018). Credibility of sustainability reports: The contribution of audit committees. *Business Strategy and the Environment*, 27(7), 973–986.

Amore, M. D., Garofalo, O., & Minichilli, A. (2014). Gender interactions within the family firm. *Management Science*, 60(5), 1083–1097.

Amran, A., Lee, S. P., & Devi, S. S. (2014). The influence of governance structure and strategic corporate social responsibility toward sustainability reporting quality. *Business Strategy and the Environment*, 23(4), 217–235.

Apesteguia, J., Azmat, G., & Iriberri, N. (2012). The impact of gender composition on team performance and decision-making: Evidence from the field. *Management Science*, 58(1), 78–93.

Arayssi, M., Dah, M., & Jizi, M. (2016). Women on boards, sustainability reporting and firm performance. *Sustainability Accounting, Management and Policy Journal*, 7(3), 376–401.

Armstrong, C. S., Core, J. E., & Guay, W. R. (2014). Do independent directors cause improvements in firm transparency? *Journal of Financial Economics*, 113(3), 383–403.

Avaredo, F., Chancel, L., Piketty, T., Sáez E., & Zucman, G. (Eds.) (2018). World Inequality Report.

Baron, R. A., & Henry, R. A. (2011). Entrepreneurship: The genesis of organizations. In S. Zedeck (Ed.), *APA Handbook of Industrial and Organizational Psychology* (Vol. 1, pp. 241–273). Washington, DC: APA.

Baumgärtner, S. (2006). Measuring the diversity of what? And for what purpose? A conceptual comparison of ecological and economic biodiversity indices. Available at: https://ssrn.com/abstract=894782

Bear, S., Rahman, N., & Post, C. (2010). The impact of board diversity and gender composition on corporate social responsibility and firm reputation. *Journal of Business Ethics*, 97(2), 207–221.

Becker, G. S. (1993). *Human capital*. Chicago, IL: The University of Chicago Press.

Ben Barka, H., & Dardour, A. (2015). Investigating the relationship between director's profile, board interlocks and corporate social responsibility. *Management Decision*, 53(3), 553–570.

Bernardi, R. A., Bosco, S. M., & Columb, V. L. (2009). Does female representation on boards of directors associate with the 'most ethical companies' list? *Corporate Reputation Review*, 12(3), 270–280.

Bertrand, M., & Hallock, K. (2000). The gender gap in top corporate jobs. NBER Working Paper Series.

Bilimoria, D. (2006). The relationship between women corporate directors and women corporate officers. *Journal of Managerial Issues*, 18(1), 47–61.

Birley, S., Cromie, S., & Myers, A. (1990). Entrepreneurial networks: Their emergence in Ireland and overseas. *International Small Business Journal*, 9(4), 56–74.

Blau, P. M. (1977). *Inequality and heterogeneity: A primitive theory of social structure*. New York: Free Press.

Blum, T. C., Fields, D. L., & Goodman, J. S. (1994). Organization-level determinants of women in management. *Academy of Management Journal*, 37(2), 241–268.

Boffey, D. (2017). "UK gender inequality as bad as 10 years ago, EU league table shows", in *The Guardian*, 11 October. Available at: www.theguardian.com/inequality/2017/oct/11/ukno-further-forward-on-tacklinggender-inequality-eu-leaguetable-shows

Bøhren, Ø., & Staubo, S. (2014). Does mandatory gender balance work? Changing organizational form to avoid board upheaval. Journal of Corporate Finance, 28, 152–168.

Bøhren, Ø., & Strøm, R. Ø. (2010). Governance and politics: Regulating independence and diversity in the board room. *Journal of Business Finance and Accounting*, 37(9–10), 1281–1308.

Brammer, S., Williams, G., & Zinkin, J. (2007). Religion and attitudes to corporate social responsibility in a large cross-country sample. *Journal of Business Ethics*, 71, 229–243.

Bravo, F., & Alcaide-Ruiz, M. D. (2019). The disclosure of financial forward-looking information: Does the financial expertise of female directors make a difference? *Gender in Management: An International Journal*, 34(2), 140–156.

Bravo, F., & Reguera-Alvarado, N. (2019). Sustainable development disclosure: Environmental, social, and governance reporting and gender diversity in the audit committee. *Business Strategy and the Environment*, 28(2), 418–429.

Brush, C. G. (1992). Research on women business owners: Past trends, a new perspective and future research directions. *Entrepreneurship, Theory and Practice*, 16(4), 5–26.

Brush, C. G., De Bruin, A., & Welter, F. (2009). A gender-aware framework for women's entrepreneurship. *International Journal of Gender and Entrepreneurship*, 1(1), 8–24.

Burke, R. J. (1997). Women on corporate boards of directors: A needed resource. *Journal of Business Ethics*, 16(9), 909–915.

Buttner, E. H., & Moore, D. P. (1997). Women's organizational exodus to entrepreneurship: Self-reported motivations and correlates with success. *Journal of Small Business Management*, 35, 34–46.

Byron, K., & Post, C. (2016). Women on boards of directors and corporate social performance: A meta-analysis. *Corporate Governance: An International Review*, 24(4), 428–442.

Cabrera-Fernández, A. I., Martínez-Jiménez, R., & Hernández-Ortiz, M. J. (2016). Women's participation on boards of directors: A review of the literature. *International Journal of Gender and Entrepreneurship*, 8(1), 69–89.

Campbell, K., & Mínguez-Vera, A. (2008). Gender diversity in the boardroom and firm financial performance. *Journal of Business Ethics*, 83(3), 435–451.

Carcello, J. V., Hollingsworth, C. W., Klein, A., & Neal, T. L. (2006). Audit committee financial expertise, competing corporate governance mechanisms, and earnings management. Available at: https://ssrn.com/abstract=887512

Carrasco, A., & Francoeur, C. (2018). Mimetic isomorphism of board gender diversity in the world. In L. E. Devnew, M. J. Le Ber, M. Torchia, & R. J. Burke (Eds.), *More Women on Boards: An International Perspective* (pp. 51–68). Charlotte, NC: Information Age Publishing.

Carrasco, A., Francoeur, C., Labelle, R., Laffarga, J., & Ruiz-Barbadillo, E. (2015). Appointing women to boards: Is there a cultural bias? *Journal of Business Ethics*, 129(2), 429–444.

Carrasco, A., & Laffarga, J. (2006). Códigos del Buen Gobierno y Diversidad. *AECA: Revista de la Asociación española de Contabilidad y Administración de empresas*, 76, 48–52.

Carrera, N., Gutierrez, I., & Carmona, S. (2001). Gender, the state and the audit profession: Evidence from Spain (1942–88). *European Accounting Review*, 10(4), 803–815.

Carter, D. A., Simkins, B. J., & Simpson, W. G. (2003). Corporate governance, board diversity, and firm value. *Financial Review*, 38(1), 33–53.

Carton, A. M., & Rosette A. S. (2011). Explaining bias against black leaders: Integrating theory on information processing and goal-based stereotyping. *Academy of Management Journal*, 54(6), 1141–1158.

Chambers, N., Harvey, G., Mannion, R., Bond, J., & Marshall, J. (2013). Towards a framework for enhancing the performance of NHS boards: A synthesis of the evidence about board governance, board effectiveness and board development. *Health Services and Delivery Research*, 1(6).

Chen, G., Crossland, C., & Huang, S. (2016). Female board representation and corporate acquisition intensity. *Strategic Management Journal*, 37(2), 303–313.

Chen, G., Liu, C., & Tjosvold, D. (2005). Conflict management for effective top management teams and innovation in China. *Journal of Management Studies*, 42, 277–300.

Chen, J., Leung, W. S., & Goergen, M. (2017). The impact of board gender composition on dividend payouts. *Journal of Corporate Finance*, 43, 86–105.

Cheng, B., Ioannou, I., & Serafeim, G. (2014). Corporate social responsibility and access to finance. *Strategic Management Journal*, 35(1), 1–23.

Cook, A., & Glass, C. (2016). Do women advance equity? The effect of gender leadership composition on LGBT-friendly policies in American firms. *Human Relations*, 69(7), 1431–1456.

Croson, R., & Gneezy, U. (2009). Gender differences in preferences. *Journal of Economic Literature*, 47(2), 1–27.

Cuomo, F., Mallin, C., & Zattoni, A. (2016). Corporate governance codes: A review and research agenda. *Corporate Governance: An International Review*, 24(3), 222–241.

Data Morphosis (2019). Gender Map: Global. Retrieved from http://town.com/gendermap/#/economy/groupBy/country/detail.

Daily, C. M., Dalton, D. R., & Cannella Jr, A. A. (2003). Corporate governance: Decades of dialogue and data. *Academy of Management Review*, 28(3), 371–382.

Dallas, L. L. (2002). The New Managerialism and Diversity on Corporate Boards of Directors. Public Law and Legal Theory Working Paper 38 (Spring). University of San Diego School of Law.

Davis, J. H., Schoorman, F. D., & Donaldson, L. (1997). Davis, Schoorman, and Donaldson reply: The distinctiveness of agency theory and stewardship theory. *The Academy of Management Review*, 22(3), 611–613.

Dawar, G., & Singh, S. (2016). Corporate social responsibility and gender diversity: A literature review. *Journal of IMS Group*, 13(1), 61–71.

Detthamrong, U., Chancharat, N., & Vithessonthi, C. (2017). Corporate governance, capital structure and firm performance: Evidence from Thailand. *Research in International Business and Finance*, 42, 689–709.

Dezso, C. L., & Ross, D. G. (2012). Does female representation in top management improve firm performance? A panel data investigation. *Strategic Management Journal*, 33(9), 1072–1089.

Díaz-García, C., González-Moreno, A., & Jose Sáez-Martínez, F. (2013). Gender diversity within R&D teams: Its impact on radicalness of innovation. *Innovation*, 15(2), 149–160.

Dissart, J. C. (2003). Regional economic diversity and regional economic stability: Research results and agenda. *International Regional Science Review*, 26(4), 423–446.

Dorius, S. F., & Firebaugh, G. (2010). Trends in global gender inequality. *Social Forces*, 88(5), 1941–1968.

Dou, Y., Sahgal, S., & Zhang, E. J. (2015). Should independent directors have term limits? The role of experience in corporate governance. *Financial Management*, 44(3), 583–621.

Du Rietz, A., & Henrekson, M. (2000). Testing the female underperformance hypothesis. *Small Business Economics*, 14(1), 1–10.

Eagly, A. H., Johannesen-Schmidt, M. C., & Van Engen, M. L. (2003). Transformational, transactional, and laissez-faire leadership styles: A meta-analysis comparing women and men. *Psychological Bulletin*, 129(4), 569–591.

Eagly, A. H., & Johnson, B. T. (1990). Gender and leadership style: A meta-analysis. *Psychological Bulletin*, 108(2), 233–256.

EIGE (2016). Gender in entrepreneurship. European Institute for Gender Equality.

Elkinawy, S., & Stater, M. (2011). Gender differences in executive compensation: Variation with board gender composition and time. *Journal of Economics and Business*, 63(1), 23–45.

Elstad, B., & Ladegard, G. (2012). Women on corporate boards: Key influencers or tokens? *Journal of Management and Governance*, 16(4), 595–615.

Ely, R. J. (2004). A field study of group diversity, participation in diversity education programs, and performance. *Journal of Organizational Behavior*, 25(6), 755–780.

European Commission (2001). Commission des Communautés Européennes Livre vert. Promouvoir un cadre européen pour la responsabilité sociale des entreprises.

European Commission (2012). Women in economic decision-making in the EU. Progress report. A Europe 2020 initiative. EU Publications.

European Commission (2018). Report on equality between women and men in the EU. EU Publications.

European Commission (2019). Gender pay gap statistics. Available at: https://ec.europa.eu/eurostat/statistics-explained/index.php/Gender_pay_gap_statistics

Fama, E. F., & Jensen, M. C. (1983). Separation of ownership and control. *Journal of Law and Economics*, 26(2), 301–325.

Farrell, K. A., & Hersch, P. L. (2005). Additions to corporate boards: The effect of gender. *Journal of Corporate Finance*, 11(1–2), 85–106.

Fortune (2018). The Most Powerful Women in Business. Available at: https://fortune.com/2018/09/24/fortune-most-powerful-women-methodology-2018/

Francoeur, C., Labelle, R., & Sinclair-Desgagné, B. (2008). Gender diversity in corporate governance and top management. *Journal of Business Ethics*, 81(1), 83–95.

Fraser-Moleketi, G. J., & Mizrahi, S. (2015). Where are the women: Inclusive boardrooms in Africa's top listed companies? African Development Bank.

Freeman, R. E., Harrison, J. S., Wicks, A. C., Parmar, B. L., & De Colle, S. (2010). *Stakeholder theory*. Cambridge: Cambridge University Press.

Fryxell, G. E., & Lerner, L. D. (1989). Contrasting corporate profiles: Women and minority representation in top management positions. *Journal of Business Ethics*, 8, 341–352.

Galbreath, J. (2018). Do boards of directors influence corporate sustainable development? An attention-based analysis. *Business Strategy and the Environment*, 27(6), 742–756.

Galia, F., & Zenou, E. (2012). Board composition and forms of innovation: Does diversity make a difference? *European Journal of International Management*, 6(6), 630–650.

Garcia-Castro, R., Ariño, M., & Canela, M. (2010). Does social performance really lead to financial performance? Accounting for endogeneity. *Journal of Business Ethics*, 92, 107–126.

García-Meca, E., & Palacio, C. J. (2018). Board composition and firm reputation: The role of business experts, support specialists and community influentials. *Business Research Quarterly*, 21(2), 111–123.

German Stock Corporation Act (2016). Introductory Law of the German Stock Corporation Act.

Giles, O. A., & Murphy, D. (2016). SLAPPed: The relationship between SLAPP suits and changed ESG reporting by firms. *Sustainability Accounting, Management and Policy Journal*, 7(1), 44–79.

Glass, C., Cook, A., & Ingersoll, A. R. (2016). Do women leaders promote sustainability? Analyzing the effect of corporate governance composition on environmental performance. *Business Strategy and the Environment*, 25(7), 495–511.

Gregory-Smith, I., Main, B. G., & O'Reilly III, C. A. (2014). Appointments, pay and performance in UK boardrooms by gender. *The Economic Journal*, 124(574), F109–F128.

Grosvold, J., Brammer, S., & Rayton, B. (2007). Board diversity in the United Kingdom and Norway: An exploratory analysis. *Business Ethics: European Review*, 16, 344–357.

Grosvold, J., & Brammer, S. (2011). National institutional systems as antecedents of female board representation: An empirical study. *Corporate Governance: An International Review*, 19(2), 116–135.

Grosvold, J., Rayton, B., & Brammer, S. (2016). Women on corporate boards: A comparative institutional analysis. *Business and Society*, 55(8), 1157–1196.

Gul, F. A., Srinidhi, B., & Ng, A. C. (2011). Does board gender diversity improve the informativeness of stock prices? *Journal of Accounting and Economics*, 51(3), 314–338.

Gull, A. A., Nekhili, M., Nagati, H., & Chtioui, T. (2018). Beyond gender diversity: How specific attributes of female directors affect earnings management. *The British Accounting Review*, 50(3), 255–274.

Harjoto, M., Laksmana, I., & Lee, R. (2015). Board diversity and corporate social responsibility. *Journal of Business Ethics*, 132(4), 641–660.

Harrigan, K. R. (1981). Numbers and positions of women elected to corporate boards. *Academy of Management Journal*, 24, 619–625.

Harrison, D. A., & Klein, K. J. (2007). What's the difference? Diversity constructs as separation, variety, or disparity in organizations. *Academy of Management Review*, 32(4), 1199–1228.

Haynes, K. (2008). Moving the gender agenda or stirring chicken's entrails? Where next for feminist methodologies in accounting? *Accounting, Auditing and Accountability Journal*, 21(4), 539–555.

Haynes, K. (2017). Accounting as gendering and gendered: A review of 25 years of critical accounting research on gender. *Critical Perspectives on Accounting*, 43, 110–124.

Helfaya, A., & Moussa, T. (2017). Do board's corporate social responsibility strategy and orientation influence environmental sustainability disclosure? UK evidence. *Business Strategy and the Environment*, 26(8), 1061–1077.

Heminway, J. M. (2007). Sex, trust, and corporate boards. *Hastings Women's LJ*, 18, 173.

Henderson, S. L., & Jeydel, A. S. (2014). Women and international politics. *Women and politics in a global world* (pp. 20–21). New York: Oxford University Press.

Herfindahl, O. C. (1950). Concentration in the US steel industry. Unpublished doctoral dissertation, Columbia University, New York.

Hillman, A. J. (2015). Board diversity: Beginning to unpeel the onion. *Corporate Governance: An International Review*, 23(2), 104–107.

Hillman, A. J., Cannella Jr, A. A., & Harris, I. C. (2002). Women and racial minorities in the boardroom: How do directors differ? *Journal of Management*, 28(6), 747–763.

Hillman, A. J., & Dalziel, T. (2003). Boards of directors and firm performance: Integrating agency and resource dependence perspectives. *Academy of Management Review*, 28(3), 383–396.

Hirschman, A. O. (1964). The paternity of an index. *American Economic Review*, 54, 761–762.

Hofstede, G. (1980). *Culture's consequences*. Beverly Hills, CA: Sage Publications.

Horbach, J., & Jacob, J. (2018). The relevance of personal characteristics and gender diversity for (eco-) innovation activities at the firm-level: Results from a linked employer–employee database in Germany. *Business Strategy and the Environment*, 27(7), 924–934.

Horwitz, S. K., & Horwitz, I. B. (2007). The effects of team diversity on team outcomes: A meta-analytic review of team demography. *Journal of Management*, 33(6), 987–1015.

Ibarra, H., & Smith-Lovin, L. (1997). New directions in social network research on gender and organizational careers. *Creating Tomorrow's Organization*, 359–383.

Inglehart, R., Norris, P., & Ronald, I. (2003). *Rising tide: Gender equality and cultural change around the world*. Cambridge: Cambridge University Press.

Ioannou, I., & Serafeim, G. (2015). The impact of corporate social responsibility on investment recommendations: Analysts' perceptions and shifting institutional logics. *Strategic Management Journal*, 36(7), 1053–1081.

Isidro, H., & Sobral, M. (2015). The effects of women on corporate boards on firm value, financial performance, and ethical and social compliance. *Journal of Business Ethics*, 132(1), 1–19.

Jeacle, I. (2011). A practice of her own: Female career success beyond the accounting firm. *Critical Perspectives on Accounting*, 22(3), 288–303.

Jensen, M. C., & Meckling, W. H. (1976). Theory of the firm: Managerial behavior, agency costs and ownership structure. *Journal of Financial Economics*, 3(4), 305–360.

Joecks, J., Pull, K., & Vetter, K. (2013). Gender diversity in the boardroom and firm performance: What exactly constitutes a "critical mass"? *Journal of Business Ethics*, 118(1), 61–72.

Johnson, S. G., Schnatterly, K., & Hill, A. D. (2013). Board composition beyond independence: Social capital, human capital, and demographics. *Journal of Management*, 39(1), 232–262.

Joshi, A., Liao, H., & Roh, H. (2011). Bridging domains in workplace demography research: A review and reconceptualization. *Journal of Management*, 37(2), 521–552.

Joshi, A., Neely, B., Emrich, C., Griffiths, D., & George, G. (2015). Gender research in *AMJ*: An overview of five decades of empirical research and calls to action. Thematic issue on gender in management research. *Academy of Management Journal*, 58(5), 1459–1475.

Kaijser, A., & Kronsell, A. (2014). Climate change through the lens of intersectionality. *Environmental Politics*, 23(3), 417–433.

Kanter, R. M. (1977). *Men and women of the corporation*. New York: Basic Books.

Kim, D., & Starks, L. T. (2016). Gender diversity on corporate boards: Do women contribute unique skills? *American Economic Review*, 106(5), 267–271.

Kiradjian, F. (2018). Women on boards: Why the conversation matters. Available at: www.forbes.com/sites/forbeslacouncil/2018/05/21/women-on-boards-why-the-conversation-matters/#1fe870c73a50

Kirsch, A. (2018). The gender composition of corporate boards: A review and research agenda. *The Leadership Quarterly*, 29(2), 346–364.

Kochan, T., Bezrukova, K., Ely, R., Jackson, S., Joshi, A., Jehn, K., Leonard, J., Levine, D., & Thomas, D. (2003). The effects of diversity on business performance: Report of the diversity research network. *Human Resource Management*, 42(1), 3–21.

Konrad, A. M., Kramer, V., & Erkut, S. (2008). Critical mass: The impact of three or more women on corporate boards. *Organizational Dynamics*, 37(2), 145–164.

Kramer, V., Konrad, A., & Erkut, S. (2006). Critical Mass on Corporate Boards: Why Three or More Women Enhance Governance. Report No. WCW 11, Wellesley Centers for Women, Wellesley, MA.

Krishnan, H. A., & Park, D. (2005). A few good women—on top management teams. *Journal of Business Research*, 58(12), 1712–1720.

Kumar, P., & Zattoni, A. (2016) Corporate governance, board gender diversity and firm performance. *Corporate Governance: An International Review*, 24, 388–389. https://doi.org/10.1111/corg.12172

Labelle, R., Francoeur, C., & Lakhal, F. (2015). To regulate or not to regulate? Early evidence on the means used around the world to promote gender diversity in the boardroom. *Gender, Work and Organization*, 22(4), 339–363.

Lanis, R., Richardson, G., & Taylor, G. (2017). Board of director gender and corporate tax aggressiveness: An empirical analysis. *Journal of Business Ethics*, 144(3), 577–596.

Larcker, D. F., & Rusticus, T. O. (2010). On the use of instrumental variables in accounting research. *Journal of Accounting and Economics*, 49(3), 186–205.

Lau, D. C., & Murnighan, J. K. (1998). Demographic diversity and faultlines: The compositional dynamics of organizational groups. *Academy of Management Review*, 23(2), 325–340.

Law n° 2014–873, August 2014. Pour l'égalité réelle entre les femmes et les hommes. Available at: www.legifrance.gouv.fr/affichTexte.do?cidTexte=JOR FTEXT000029330832&categorieLien=id

Law 62/2017, August 1. Regime da representação equilibrada entre mulheres e homens nos órgãos de administração e de fiscalização das entidades do setor público empresarial e das empresas cotadas em bolsa. Available at: https://data.dre.pt/eli/lei/62/2017/08/01/p/dre/pt/html

Levi, M., Li, K., & Zhang, F. (2014). Director gender and mergers and acquisitions. *Journal of Corporate Finance*, 28, 185–200.

Li, J., Zhao, F., Chen, S., Jiang, W., Liu, T., & Shi, S. (2017). Gender diversity on boards and firms' environmental policy. *Business Strategy and the Environment*, 26(3), 306–315.

Liao, L., Luo, L., & Tang, Q. (2015). Gender diversity, board independence, environmental committee and greenhouse gas disclosure. *The British Accounting Review*, 47(4), 409–424.

Lieberson, S. (1969). Measuring population diversity. American Sociological Review, 34(6), 850–862.

Liu, Y., Wei, Z., & Xie, F. (2014). Do women directors improve firm performance in China? *Journal of Corporate Finance*, 28, 169–184.

Lord, C. G., & Saenz, D. S. (1985). Memory deficits and memory surfeits: Differential cognitive consequences of tokenism for tokens and observers. *Journal of Personality and Social Psychology*, 49(4), 918–926.

Low, D. C., Roberts, H., & Whiting, R. H. (2015). Board gender diversity and firm performance: Empirical evidence from Hong Kong, South Korea, Malaysia and Singapore. *Pacific-Basin Finance Journal*, 35, 381–401.

Lucas-Pérez, M. E., Mínguez-Vera, A., Baixauli-Soler, J. S., Martín-Ugedo, J. F., & Sánchez-Marín, G. (2015). Women on the board and managers' pay: Evidence from Spain. *Journal of Business Ethics*, 129(2), 265–280.

Madhani, P. M. (2017). Diverse roles of corporate board: Review of various corporate governance theories. *IUP Journal of Corporate Governance*, 16(2), 7–28.

Main, B. G., & Gregory-Smith, I. (2018). Symbolic management and the glass cliff: Evidence from the boardroom careers of female and male directors. *British Journal of Management*, 29(1), 136–155.

Man, C. K., & Wong, B. (2013). Corporate governance and earnings management: A survey. *Journal of Applied Business Research*, 29(2), 391–418.

Manita, R., Bruna, M. G., Dang, R., & Houanti, L. H. (2018). Board gender diversity and ESG disclosure: Evidence from the USA. *Journal of Applied Accounting Research*, 19(2), 206–224.

McKinsey Global Institute (2015). The power of parity: How advancing women's equality can add $12 trillion to global growth.

McKinsey Global Institute (2018). Women in the workplace 2018.

McNamara, C. (2001). *Overview of roles and responsibilities of corporate board of directors*. Free Management Library.

Mensi-Klarbach, H. (2014). Gender in top management research: Towards a comprehensive research framework. *Management Research Review*, 37(6), 538–552.

Meyer, J. W., & Rowan, B. (1977). Institutionalized organizations: Formal structure as myth and ceremony. *American Journal of Sociology*, 83(2), 340–363.

Miller, T., & del Carmen Triana, M. (2009). Demographic diversity in the boardroom: Mediators of the board diversity–firm performance relationship. *Journal of Management Studies*, 46(5), 755–786.

Moore, D. P., & Buttner, E. H. (1997). *Women entrepreneurs: Moving beyond the glass ceiling*. Thousand Oaks, CA: Sage Publications.

Morrison, A. M., White, R. P., Van Velsor, E., & Center for Creative Leadership (1987). *Breaking the glass ceiling*. Reading, MA: Addison-Wesley.

Niederle, M., & Vesterlund, L. (2007). Do women shy away from competition? Do men compete too much? *Quarterly Journal of Economics*, 122(3), 1067–1101.

Nielsen, S., & Huse, M. (2010). The contribution of women on boards of directors: Going beyond the surface. *Corporate Governance: An International Review*, 18(2), 136–148.

Oakley, J. G. (2000). Gender-based barriers to senior management positions: Understanding the scarcity of female CEOs. *Journal of Business Ethics*, 27(4), 321–334.

Organisation for Economic Co-operation and Development (OECD) (2019). Share of employed who are own-account workers, by sex. Available at: www.oecd.org/gender/data/shareofemployedwhoareown-accountworkersbygender.htm

Pan, Y., & Sparks, J. R. (2012). Predictors, consequence, and measurement of ethical judgments: Review and meta-analysis. *Journal of Business Research*, 65(1), 84–91.

Pelled, L. H. (1996). Demographic diversity, conflict, and work group outcomes: An intervening process theory. Organization Science, 7(6), 615–631.

Perrault, E. (2015). Why does board gender diversity matter and how do we get there? The role of shareholder activism in deinstitutionalizing old boys' networks. *Journal of Business Ethics*, 128(1), 149–165.

Pfeffer, J., & Salancik, G. R. (1978). *The external control of organizations: A resource dependence perspective*. New York: Harper and Row.

Portes, A. (1998). Social capital. *Annual Review of Sociology*, 24, 1–24.

Powell, M., & Ansic, D. (1997). Gender differences in risk behaviour in financial decision-making: An experimental analysis. *Journal of Economic Psychology*, 18(6), 605–628.

Pucheta-Martínez, M. C., Bel-Oms, I., & Olcina-Sempere, G. (2016). Corporate governance, female directors and quality of financial information. *Business Ethics: A European Review*, 25(4), 363–385.

Pugliese, A., Bezemer, P. J., Zattoni, A., Huse, M., Van den Bosch, F. A., & Volberda, H. W. (2009). Boards of directors' contribution to strategy: A literature review and research agenda. *Corporate Governance: An International Review*, 17(3), 292–306.

Quintana-García, C., & Benavides-Velasco, C. A. (2016). Gender diversity in top management teams and innovation capabilities: The initial public offerings of biotechnology firms. *Long Range Planning*, 49(4), 507–518.

Rao, K., Tilt, C. A., & Lester, L. H. (2012). Corporate governance and environmental reporting: An Australian study. *Corporate Governance: The International Journal of Business in Society*, 12(2), 143–163.

Rao, K., & Tilt, C. (2016). Board diversity and CSR reporting: An Australian study. *Meditari Accountancy Research*, 24(2), 182–210.

Real Decreto-ley 6/2019, March 1. Medidas urgentes para garantía de la igualdad de trato y de oportunidades entre mujeres y hombres en el empleo y la ocupación. Available at: www.boe.es/eli/es/rdl/2019/03/01/6/con

Reguera-Alvarado, N., de Fuentes, P., & Laffarga, J. (2017). Does board gender diversity influence financial performance? Evidence from Spain. *Journal of Business Ethics*, 141(2), 337–350.

Reguera-Alvarado, N., & Bravo, F. (2018). The impact of directors' high-tech experience on innovation in low-tech firms. *Innovation*, 20(3), 223–239.

Rhode, D. L., & Packel, A. K. (2014). Diversity on corporate boards: How much difference does difference make. *Del. J. Corp. L.*, 39, 377.

Richard, O. C. (2000). Racial diversity, business strategy, and firm performance: A resource-based view. *Academy of Management Journal*, 43(2), 164–177.

Ritter-Hayashi, D., Vermeulen, P., & Knoben, J. (2016). Gender diversity and innovation: The role of women's economic opportunity in developing countries. Tilburg University. Available at: www.tilburguniversity.edu/dfid-innovation-and-growth

Rivas, J. L. (2012). Diversity and internationalization: The case of boards and TMT's. *International Business Review*, 21(1), 1–12.

Roberson, Q. M., & Park, H. J. (2007). Examining the link between diversity and firm performance: The effects of diversity reputation and leader racial diversity. *Group and Organization Management*, 32(5), 548–568.

Robinson, G., & Dechant, K. (1997). Building a business case for diversity. *Academy of Management Executive*, 11(3), 21–31.

Rose, C. (2007). Does female board representation influence firm performance? The Danish evidence. *Corporate Governance: An International Review*, 15(2), 404–413.

Rosette, A. S., Leonardelli, G. J., & Phillips, K. W. (2008). The white standard: Racial bias in leader categorization. *Journal of Applied Psychology*, 93(4), 758–777.

Ryan, M. K., & Haslam, S. A. (2005). The glass cliff: Evidence that women are over-represented in precarious leadership positions. *British Journal of Management*, 16(2), 81–90.

Shackleton, K. (1999). Gender segregation in Scottish chartered accountancy: The deployment of male concerns about the admission of women, 1900–25. *Accounting, Business and Financial History*, 9(1), 135–156.

Sheridan, A., & Milgate, G. (2005). Accessing board positions: A comparison of female and male board members' views. *Corporate Governance: An International Review*, 13, 847–855.

Shleifer, A., & Vishny, R. W. (1997). A survey of corporate governance. *Journal of Finance*, 52(2), 737–783.

Siciliano, J. I. (1996). The relationship of board member diversity to organizational performance. *Journal of Business Ethics*, 15(12), 1313–1320.

Sila, V., Gonzalez, A., & Hagendorff, J. (2016). Women on board: Does boardroom gender diversity affect firm risk? *Journal of Corporate Finance*, 36, 26–53.

Simpson, E. H. (1949). Measurement of diversity. *Nature*, 163, 688.

Singh, V., & Vinnicombe, S. (2004). Why so few women in top UK boardrooms? Evidence and theoretical explanations. *Corporate Governance: An International Review*, 12, 479–488.

Skaggs, S., Stainback, K., & Duncan, P. (2012). Shaking things up or business as usual? The influence of female corporate executives and board of directors on women's managerial representation. *Social Science Research*, 41(4), 936–948.

Smith, N., Smith, V., & Verner, M. (2006). Do women in top management affect firm performance? A panel study of 2,500 Danish firms. *International Journal of Productivity and Performance Management*, 55(7), 569–593.

Solow, A. R., & Polasky, S. (1994). Measuring biological diversity. Environmental and Ecological Statistics, 1(2), 95–103.

Spencer Stuart (2018). Board index.

Srinidhi, B., Gul, F. A., & Tsui, J. (2011). Female directors and earnings quality. *Contemporary Accounting Research*, 28(5), 1610–1644.

Stasser, G., & Birchmeier, Z. (2003). Group creativity and collective choice. In P. B. Paulus & B. A. Nijstad (Eds.), *Group creativity: Innovation through collaboration* (pp. 85–109). Oxford: Oxford University Press.

Stirling, A. (1998). On the Economics and Analysis of Diversity. Science Policy Research Unit Electronic Working Paper Series, Paper no. 28, University of Sussex.

Sullivan, D. M., & Meek, W. R. (2012). Gender and entrepreneurship: A review and process model. *Journal of Managerial Psychology*, 27(5), 428–458.

Tejedo-Romero, F., Rodrigues, L. L., & Craig, R. (2017). Women directors and disclosure of intellectual capital information. *European Research on Management and Business Economics*, 23(3), 123–131.

Terjesen, S., Aguilera, R. V., & Lorenz, R. (2015). Legislating a woman's seat on the board: Institutional factors driving gender quotas for boards of directors. *Journal of Business Ethics*, 128(2), 233–251.

Terjesen, S., Sealy, R., & Singh, V. (2009). Women directors on corporate boards: A review and research agenda. *Corporate Governance: An International Review*, 17, 320–337.

Terjesen, S., & Sealy, R. (2016). Board gender quotas: Exploring ethical tensions from a multi-theoretical perspective. *Business Ethics Quarterly*, 26(1), 23–65.

Thorne, L., Massey, D. W., & Magnan, M. (2003). Institutional context and auditors' moral reasoning: A Canada-US comparison. *Journal of Business Ethics*, 43(4), 305–321.

Torchia, M., Calabrò, A., & Huse, M. (2011). Women directors on corporate boards: From tokenism to critical mass. *Journal of Business Ethics*, 102(2), 299–317.

Triana, M. D. C., Miller, T. L., & Trzebiatowski, T. M. (2013). The double-edged nature of board gender diversity: Diversity, firm performance, and the power of women directors as predictors of strategic change. *Organization Science*, 25(2), 609–632.

Tripathi, A., & Bains, A. (2013). Evolution of corporate social responsibility: A journey from 1700 BC till 21st century. *International Journal of Advanced Research*, 1(8), 788–796.

Ujunwa, A. (2012). Board characteristics and the financial performance of Nigerian quoted firms. *Corporate Governance: The International Journal of Business in Society*, 12(5), 656–674.

United Nations (2011). Resolution adopted by the General Assembly on 19 December 2011.

United Nations Women (2014). Annual report, 2014–2015. New York: UN Women. Available at: http://annualreport.unwomen.org/en/2015.

Van der Vegt, G. S., & Janssen, O. (2003). Joint impact of interdependence and group diversity on innovation. *Journal of Management*, 29(5), 729–751.

Verbeek, M. (2008). *A guide to modern econometrics* (2nd ed.). Chichester: Wiley and Sons.

Westphal, J. D., & Bednar, M. K. (2005). Pluralistic ignorance in corporate boards and firms' strategic persistence in response to low firm performance. *Administrative Science Quarterly*, 50(2), 262–298.

Westphal, J. D., & Milton, L. P. (2000). How experience and network ties affect the influence of demographic minorities on corporate boards. *Administrative Science Quarterly*, 45, 366–398.

Westphal, J. D., & Stern, I. (2007). Flattery will get you everywhere (especially if you are a male Caucasian): How integration, boardroom behaviour, and demographic minority status affect additional board appointments at US companies. *Academy of Management Journal*, 50, 267–288.

Westphal, J. D., & Zajac, E. J. (1995). Who shall govern? CEO board power, demographic similarity, and new director selection. *Administrative Science Quarterly*, 40(1), 60–83.

Williams, K. Y., & O'Reilly III, C. A. (1998). Demography and diversity in organizations: A review of 40 years of research. In B. M. Staw & L. L. Cummings (Eds.), *Research in organizational behavior* (Vol. 20, pp. 77–140). Stamford, CT: JAI.

Wilson, T. E. (2014). Gender board diversity: Further evidence on women in corporate governance. *Journal of Finance and Accountancy*, 16, 1.

Wood, W., & Eagly, A. H. (2009). Gender identity. In M. R. Leary & R. H. Howe (Eds.), *Handbook of individual differences in social behavior* (pp. 109–125). New York: Guilford Press.

World Economic Forum (2016). The industry gender gap women and work in the fourth industrial revolution.

Zapalska, A. (1997). A profile of women entrepreneurs and enterprises in Poland. *Journal of Small Business Management*, 35(4), 76–82.

Zelechowski, D. D., & Bilimoria, D. (2004). Characteristics of women and men corporate inside directors in the US. *Corporate Governance: An International Review*, 12(3), 337–342.

Zhang, J., Han, J., & Yin, M. (2018). A female style in corporate social responsibility? Evidence from charitable donations. *International Journal of Disclosure and Governance*, 15(3), 185–196.

Zhu, D. H., Shen, W., & Hillman, A. J. (2014). Recategorization into the in-group: The appointment of demographically different new directors and their subsequent positions on corporate boards. *Administrative Science Quarterly*, 59(2), 240–270.

Zona, F., Zattoni, A., & Minichilli, A. (2013). A contingency model of boards of directors and firm innovation: The moderating role of firm size. *British Journal of Management*, 24(3), 299–315.

Zucker, L. G. (1987). Institutional theories of organization. *Annual Review of Sociology*, 13(1), 443–464.

Index

Note: Page numbers in **bold** refer to tables; page numbers in *italic* refer to figures.

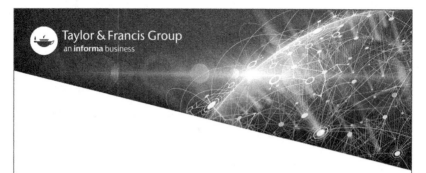

Printed in the United States
by Baker & Taylor Publisher Services